DIRECTIONAL
LIVING

DIRECTIONAL
LIVING

A Transformational Guide

to Fulfillment in Work and Life

Megan Hellerer

PENGUIN LIFE

VIKING
An imprint of Penguin Random House LLC
penguinrandomhouse.com

Copyright © 2024 by Megan Hellerer
Penguin Random House values and supports copyright. Copyright fuels
creativity, encourages diverse voices, promotes free speech, and creates a vibrant
culture. Thank you for buying an authorized edition of this book and for
complying with copyright laws by not reproducing, scanning, or distributing
any part of it in any form without permission. You are supporting writers and
allowing Penguin Random House to continue to publish books for every reader.
Please note that no part of this book may be used or reproduced in any manner
for the purpose of training artificial intelligence technologies or systems.

A Penguin Life Book

LIBRARY OF CONGRESS CATALOGING-IN-PUBLICATION DATA
Names: Hellerer, Megan, author.
Title: Directional living / Megan Hellerer.
Description: New York : Penguin Life, [2024]
Identifiers: LCCN 2024007631 (print) | LCCN 2024007632 (ebook) |
ISBN 9780593299272 (hardcover) | ISBN 9780593299289 (ebook)
Subjects: LCSH: Vocational guidance. | Quality of life.
Classification: LCC HF5381 .H3745 2024 (print) |
LCC HF5381 (ebook) | DDC 650.1—dc23/eng/20240613
LC record available at https://lccn.loc.gov/2024007631
LC ebook record available at https://lccn.loc.gov/2024007632

Printed in the United States of America
1st Printing

Designed by Cassandra Garruzzo Mueller

To me at 29,

*For having been desperate enough, and brave enough,
to abandon everything you thought you knew—
about yourself and about the world.*

Here's the guidance you were looking for and couldn't find.

To all Underfulfilled Overachievers everywhere,

*You're not alone, it's not your fault, and
you don't have to live like this.*

*There is another way and it's closer and
more attainable than you may think.*

Contents

Author's Note

Unless a full name is used, the client vignettes in this book are composites of composites and not meant to be an accurate reporting of events that occurred. While they are based on real-life experiences and actual interactions that I have had—that is to say, they are not exaggerated—the details have been materially changed to protect the privacy of my clients. My objective was to represent the essence of the personal evolution and to stay true to the spirit of the human, the work, and the relationship in each story, not to portray anything else.

DIRECTIONAL
LIVING

The Underfulfilled Overachiever

was somewhere no one ever wants to be: on the floor of a public
restroom. It was the middle of a Tuesday at Google's New York office, and I had just fled a team meeting to throw up. I didn't care about
how disgusting it was to be lying on the bathroom floor. I didn't care
about anything anymore. Shaking and dry heaving, I gripped the
sides of the toilet. I tried to count my breaths but kept losing track.

What is happening to me?!

I'd heard about a calming technique in which you methodically
try to engage all five of your senses. It had always sounded to me like
some woo-woo bullshit, but that was before I got desperate. This
wasn't my first panic attack—far from it—but it was the first time
that one had happened at work. It was the first time I couldn't manage to smile and nod my way through it.

Okay, Megan. Five things you see.

I'd turned off the fluorescent bathroom light and was lying mostly
in the dark, except for the strip of light coming in from under the
door, which was just enough for me to make out the Google logo on
my laptop.

Strip of light—super, that's one! Google logo—two.

The toilet passed for number three. The color Ballet Slippers on my manicured nails, bitten down to the quick, became number four. And the poster advertising that week's "happy"-hour concert took spot number five. How was I going to fake my "school spirit" for yet another office social event? Christ, how was I going to make it all the way to Friday?

"I can't do this anymore," I said out loud between sobs.

Get it together. Keep going. Four things you can touch.

Mascara-streaked wad of toilet paper. Puddle of tears on the tile floor. Google employee badge. The designer "luck" charm hanging from my necklace. Willing to try anything to fix my unhappiness, including jewelry, I'd splurged on it with money from my last bonus. As of yet, clearly, it wasn't helping.

"I really, really tried. I tried so hard," I whispered, aloud again, to no one at all. "How did I get here?"

Here . . . Hearing, right. Three things you can hear.

My heart beating alarmingly fast. The painful wails I couldn't believe were coming out of my own body. The whir of Googlers whizzing down the hallway on company scooters right outside the bathroom door. (Yes, it was common practice to ride scooters in between meetings for maximum transport efficiency.)

"I'm so sorry," I blurted. Who was I even apologizing to? My job? Everyone I thought I was letting down? Myself?

Almost done. Two things you can smell.

Vomit. (Gross.) Cheap bathroom air freshener. (Oh my God, maybe grosser.)

"I am so fucked."

One thing you can taste.

My afternoon latte, for the second time. Yep, definitely going to throw up again.

How Did I Get Here?

Maybe you can relate. Maybe you're even reading this from your very own proverbial bathroom floor. (Why is it always a bathroom floor?!) Or maybe you're just flirting with your floor, wherever that might be, and trying to stave off the feeling that it's inevitably where things are headed. Perhaps, like me, you can't understand where things went wrong. I'd done all the "right" things. I'd checked all the boxes and worked so, so hard to get where I was. I'd taken all AP classes and gotten straight As at a top-ranked high school in New York City. I'd been the captain of the varsity soccer and softball teams and president of the athletic association. I'd won the scholar-athlete award. I'd been chosen as a peer mentor to younger students. I'd organized an annual fundraiser for research for a cure for cystic fibrosis. I'd invested in meaningful friendships and even had a kind-hearted boyfriend.

☑ *Exceptional, well-rounded student.*

I had applied to fourteen colleges and universities because I didn't know how to decide. (Difficulty making decisions was a theme of mine.) I was accepted into many of them. I chose Stanford.

☑ *Go to the "right" college.*

In Palo Alto, I finally felt like I could let up a little. And by "let up," I mean limiting my all-nighters to once a week and graduating with a 3.9 GPA. I had a place staked out in the basement of the library and frequented it so much that I referred to it as "my" spot.

The library coffee baristas knew my name and my near lethally caffeinated order by heart. I fantasized about being a creative writing major but diligently discarded that vision as impractical—what would it "get" me? So I pursued an interdisciplinary international relations major instead. I spent my summers hostel-hopping solo through Europe, interning for NBC *Nightly News*, and reporting for Greenwich Village's free neighborhood newspaper, *The Village Voice*. I studied abroad for a semester (Florence, of course). I lived in a place on campus called the "Enchanted Broccoli Forest." I fell in love. I took a computer science class.

☑ Degree in something practical.

☑ A well-rounded college experience!

As my college graduation approached, I applied for a job at Google and was offered a position that paid more money than I ever imagined I'd make at twenty-two. I hadn't previously had even the slightest interest in tech and had only supremely basic coding skills, but I could get excited about the learning curve that came with being immersed in anything new. So despite desperately wanting to move back to my hometown of New York City, I started my new life on Google's "campus" in Mountain View, California, just days after graduation. Everyone seemed very impressed.

☑ Get the "good" job at the hot company with the salary and the health insurance and the matching 401(k).

I met a cute, smart fellow Stanford grad and Googler who became my boyfriend. This was convenient, as it meant we could multitask:

quality time together on our commute and at the office during lunch dates in the free gourmet Google cafés!

☑ Power couple status.

Pretty soon I was traveling business class all over the country as a "strategic partner manager." I met with C-suite clients many years my senior and got promoted a bunch of times.

☑ Busy!
☑ Important!

I got peer recognition awards and MVP awards, as well as bonuses for going "above and beyond" and having exceptional impact on particular projects.

☑ Capable and likable teammate.
☑ Exceptional employee.

When the New York office opened, I got myself relocated and landed a great apartment on the street where Carrie lived in *Sex and the City*.

☑ Score a trendy West Village apartment.
☑ Don a sleek, chic "corporate executive" wardrobe.
☑ Pretend sexism and misogyny are things of the past.
☑ Live up to your potential.
☑ Make it all look easy and effortless.

I had "made it." This was everything I'd worked so hard for, and my life looked like the epitome of success. I could tell by the way people's eyes lit up when someone introduced me. "This is Megan. She went to Stanford and works at Google." Just like that, I had their respect.

But my *self*-respect? Nonexistent.

How We Spend Our Days . . .

Back in that Google bathroom, when I finally ran out of tears, I crawled across the floor and pulled myself up onto the sink. I rinsed my mouth and rubbed hard at the lines of dried mascara running down my cheeks. I felt so pathetic. What I saw in the mirror was alarming. I'd suddenly and unintentionally lost twenty pounds over the previous few months and my Theory pencil skirt was hanging off of me. My eyes were hollow and empty and racoon-ish. "You're in serious trouble," I said to the haunted reflection in the mirror. "You are not okay. Look at you—you're dying."

When I reemerged from that bathroom, the team meeting had ended, and I did the only thing I could think of: I pretended nothing had happened. I told no one—not my boyfriend, not my best friend, not my sister, not my mentor, not the therapist I wasn't yet ready to find. This panic attack was only the most recent. There had also been the one on the corner of Fifteenth Street and Eighth Avenue at rush hour and the especially inconvenient one in the middle of a teeth cleaning at the dentist. There was the Saturday night spent hiding out on the fire escape at my friend's birthday party and the fetal-position-in-my-morning-shower anxiety waves, which had become so routine that I'd started setting my alarm fifteen minutes earlier to accommodate them.

I knew intuitively—with absolute, unwavering certainty—that this little "situation" had to be kept secret. I knew that something was deeply, unfixably wrong with me. *Look around,* I kept telling myself. *You have a coveted job at a company that's changing the world. You've already achieved every single goddamn thing you set out to. You are dripping with privilege. You have everything you could ever want or need. This is "success"! People are proud of you! You made it! If all this doesn't make you happy, then nothing will. How are you so ungrateful?! Why can't you just appreciate everything you have?! You must be broken.*

It wasn't just that I was miserable, unfulfilled, and so, so lost. I was ashamed. I hated myself for not being able to suck it up or figure it out and fix whatever was wrong with me. I absolutely could not let anyone know that I couldn't hack it in the tech world. It went against everything I believed about myself. How embarrassing that, despite being incredibly competent most of the time, I couldn't figure out what seemed like should be the simplest thing to determine: what the hell I was meant to do with my life. Everyone else seemed to know what to do with theirs.

The night after the bathroom-floor incident, I curled up in bed and tried, with the assistance of Kim Crawford Sauvignon Blanc, to process what had happened. Leaving my job felt like the only option. And at the same time, it didn't feel like a viable choice at all. Even just thinking about quitting made me feel like I would cease to exist. I could not fathom what "life after Google" might look like.

As irrational as it sounds, I've never felt, before or since, so viscerally, so physically, like I was dying. I can still summon the feeling when I close my eyes. It was like being on a plane in the worst possible turbulence. Your logical brain tells you it's fine. The pilot says it's fine. This is normal. It happens. It will pass. You know how rare plane crashes are. But your body, your nervous system, doesn't speak that language. It is convinced that this is The End, and it is panicking accordingly. I'd tried everything to make staying at Google palatable: switching roles, managers, cities; taking a sabbatical; doing less; doing more. And still, I ended up on the goddamn bathroom floor.

Annie Dillard famously wrote that "how we spend our days is, of course, how we spend our lives." So, how was it that I was actually spending my days? I was nauseated on my way to work, numb all day at the office, and barely going through the motions of connection and engagement only to race home as soon as possible so that I could collapse behind closed doors. I'd spent a large portion of my twenties in this dire state: depressed, anxious, isolated in plain sight—terrified of the big, long life I still had before me. Was I prepared to spend the rest of my life like this? Because that's the life I was building. This thought tormented me.

There was no single moment when I consciously chose. My body made the choice for me when I could no longer physically compel myself to *go* to work. I was too prideful to break down publicly—how unprofessional! But after the bathroom incident, I knew that I was going to fall apart, and so I was going to do so by myself in the privacy of my own home, thank you very much. The actual conversation in which I quit my job consisted of my mumbling something to some newish junior HR person in California about not being able to do this anymore. And so it was that I packed up my desk, transitioned my accounts, and walked away from everything I thought I was supposed to want. I left with no plan and no idea what I was going to do with my life. I just knew it could not be this.

The Not-That Experiment

In the movies, quitting your job is often portrayed as this trium-
phant moment of stick-it-to-the-man self-realization. Bridget Jones
gets to tell her smarmy boss that she'd rather take a job wiping Sad-
dam Hussein's ass. *The Devil Wears Prada*'s protagonist, Andy Sachs,
gallantly throws her ringing cell phone into a fountain in Paris as her
ruthless boss, Miranda Priestly, looks on aghast. But, for me, while
it did feel like I'd spectacularly blown up my life, I did not go out in
a blaze of glory or like a phoenix rising from the ashes. I did not as-
cend in rapture and bliss to an instantaneous state of joy and fulfillment as I'd expected. I'd long fantasized about ecstatically shouting
the news of my newfound freedom from every roof deck in New York
City. And a small part of me still wanted to do exactly that. But a
much louder part of me was *terrified*: no more income, no more health
insurance, no more 401(k). Almost immediately, I started imagining
emailing my old boss and telling him I'd made a mistake. I even
drafted several emails to this effect. *Just kidding! Take me back!*

The main problem was that my life did not cease to suck. It just
sucked in new ways. I had removed my job from the equation, but
the existential dread remained. I grew increasingly isolated, numb,
and agoraphobic. Because every time I left the house, everyone was
surely staring at me and my scarlet letter *F* for "failure." *There she
goes, the one who squandered all her potential.* Or: *Look away,
children. She's the one who had it all and still couldn't make it work.*
Or: *Beware of the irresponsible, unemployed mess!* I felt exposed
without the armor of an important-sounding title and the business
cards sporting a Google logo. Who was I without my carefully culti-
vated five-year plan? I dreaded the "So, what are you going to do

9

next?" question and avoided any social situation where I thought I might have to answer it. I was afraid of what it said about me that I "couldn't hack it." What if no one ever hired me again? What did I have to show for the last eight years? Did I even have any skills? I was deeply afraid that I was secretly lazy and that I'd never achieve anything ever again, let alone find something I cared about.

There were intense feelings of loss, too. I didn't understand how I could miss something that had made me so unhappy. What I didn't know then was that it wasn't the job itself I was mourning; it was a loss of identity, the death of my Google self. I needed to say goodbye to everything I thought I knew about myself and the world in order to move forward.

There was a small glimmer of freedom in this "failure." Yes, the thing I was most afraid of had happened: by my estimation, I'd failed at living the perfect, flawless life. I had to give up the charade; I couldn't fool anyone anymore. If I couldn't be perfect, then I might just have to be myself. And who the hell was that? I knew I needed to do something drastic to rewrite my default settings, to put some structure (I love structure!) around this transition and prevent my overwhelmed, anxiety-ridden, control-happy, perfectionist brain from sabotaging itself by seeking out the next shiny offer at the next biggest, could-be-a-unicorn start-up that came along just to assuage my fear.

The answer wasn't another career plan, though. Instead, I came up with something of an *anti*-career plan: a six-month experiment that, I reassured myself, I could easily ditch if it all went to shit. An "experiment" was an excellent container because it was a low-stakes way to commit to trying something new, where the goal was not to get it "right" but to test and learn. I had no idea what I was trying to do, but I did know what I was trying not to do. The mission of this experiment was simply *not that*, and so I called it the Not-That Experiment.

The rules were simple. No résumé updates. No job applications. No interviews. To pay my bills, I sold my Google stock, which felt wildly irresponsible, but I told myself that I'd reevaluate my financial situation when the experiment was over. As for what I *would* do during these six months? I would choose to do only things that I liked to do and that reminded me of who I was.

This proved harder than expected.

One day, early in the experiment, I had a meltdown in the tissue aisle of CVS. For the life of me, I couldn't figure out which freaking tissue-box design I liked. And I needed to know what I liked, goddammit! (Yes, this really happened.) I knew the ones I was "supposed to" like, the one my interior designer friend would pick and the one that would match another friend's chic monochrome style, but I had no idea which one *I* liked. I was stunned that every point of reference I had for choosing what resonated with *me* was outside of me. It was so backward. I sat down in the middle of the aisle (there I was on a public floor again!), squeezed my eyes shut, and searched inside myself, frantically swiping left on every external opinion that popped into my mind. Eventually, I would have to get to my own actual personal preferences, right?! But I was paralyzed. If I couldn't pick a silly tissue box, how was I going to pick a career, a partner, a life that I loved? It was like I'd somehow erased myself from my own life. I left without tissues. I'd just use toilet paper. I was done filling my life with things that didn't feel like *mine*.

This is why much of the rote advice to soul-searchers falls flat. *Follow your heart. Do what you love.* Trust me, I gladly would have if I'd known what that was.

Staying in the experiment, doing the opposite of everything I felt inclined to do, was a struggle, but this is one place where my perfectionism saved me: I stuck it out because I didn't want to fail (again).

What I was doing was "researching," though I didn't call it that at the time. I was looking for clues, from as many different perspectives and places as I could find, that would help me solve the great mystery of how to do this whole life thing more meaningfully.

So I went to museums and concerts, attended lectures at the 92nd Street Y, and took cooking classes and photography workshops. I participated in meditation retreats and recovery meetings. I learned about Ayurvedic doshas, and I worked on my adrenals and my serotonin with a naturopath. I stopped drinking. I read and watched and studied and listened to psychologists and sociologists, spiritual leaders, academics and researchers, coaches and inspirational speakers, memoirists, poets and artists, and entrepreneurs and founders, trying to understand how and when I had gotten so lost and how I might be found. Someone, somewhere, had to have a manual for how to do life "right," right? I took copious notes. Almost every book, interview, and article offered some nugget. I did *The Artist's Way* and morning pages. I got a therapist. I meditated daily. I purged my closets. And I wrote, a lot. Every day. I wrote down everything I was learning in assorted notebooks: what was maybe "working" and what wasn't.

All of it was kind of, sort of helping, and yet none of it felt like the full story. I was three months in, and I was still stuck and confused, still having panic attacks, still suffering through days when I just couldn't get out of bed. I was too far along to go back, but I still couldn't see a path forward. None of the resources out there seemed to help—like really, deeply help—therapy, psychology classes, Buddhism, energy healers, acupuncture, yoga, sleep, exercise, meditation, or medication . . . Where was the step-by-step guide, with an actionable plan and a checklist, to walk me through a career change? *Just tell me what to do and I'll do it!*

Then one night I pushed myself out of my sweatpants and attended a cocktail party fundraiser for a friend's nonprofit organization. I knew what was coming and did it anyway. And when, exactly three minutes after I arrived, someone asked me what I did, I started to launch into my usual vague response, then suddenly stopped. I was too tired. I couldn't muster the energy to do the whole performance of okayness. Instead, I did something radical: I told the truth.

Standing among a cluster of women I'd never met, I told them how miserable I had been at my "great" job. I told them how for eight years I'd tried so hard to "make it work" until I became so burned out, depressed, and anxious that I quit. With no plan.

I braced for the onslaught of judgment. Instead, they all nodded, and then they all began sharing:

That's exactly how I feel. I've never heard anyone else explain it like that before.

That's not normal?! I don't think I know anyone who doesn't *feel this way.*

I keep thinking that with the next promotion, I'll finally feel like I've made it, but I'm starting to think that's not happening.

I keep wondering how the hell I got here. I worked so hard and did all the things I was supposed to do.

I would quit my job, but I have no idea what else I would do.

I wish I had a passion that I could follow, but I just don't. Isn't it too late to start over anyway?

I wake up full of dread every single day, and I just live my life biding my time from vacation to vacation.

Let me know what you find out. I've been trying to figure out how to leave my company for three years!

I finally understood what they meant when they say "the truth will set you free." It's so annoying when a common aphorism like that turns out to be right, but I subsequently started sharing my story more openly with friends and former coworkers and anyone else I met. I also began asking people how they felt about their own work, which is when I realized that many brilliant and accomplished people were all secretly miserable in their jobs, unmotivated and uninspired, just trying to make it through the day.

I looked for terminology to describe this condition, but there was none, so I came up with my own: the Underfulfilled Overachiever, or UFOA for short.

Underfulfilled Overachiever (n.):

> 1. *A constant striver who is living a great-on-paper life, has checked all the boxes, done all the "right" things, amassed achievements and external success, yet still feels secretly dissatisfied, unfulfilled, and increasingly disconnected from their work, life, and self.*

> 2. *Someone who suffers from the foundational belief that achievement is the path to lasting fulfillment.*

A friend of a friend had started doing this thing called "coaching" as a side hustle; apparently, she'd gotten certified through an official coaching training program. It piqued my interest, though I couldn't explain why. "Coaching" seemed like a dubious career path to me. Nonetheless, I signed up for a Coaching Fundamentals course. I figured I was investing in learning a new skill set that I could apply when I returned to the corporate world and to managing teams— because yes, on many days I was still convinced that going back would be what I'd eventually end up doing.

To my complete surprise, it was there, in a poorly lit conference room in Midtown Manhattan, that I found the thing—or at least *a* thing—that reminded me of who I was. The language, the philosophy, the exercises, the strategy—it all made such intuitive sense to me. Maybe there was a framework and an approach that could help me figure out what I was doing with my life after all.

Inspired by the coaching training, I found myself creating the guidebook for living that I'd been seeking but didn't seem to exist. Originally, it was intended just for me, documenting the tools, strategies, techniques, and step-by-step processes I was uncovering to make sure I'd *never* end up in this situation again. But I also sent an email to a few friends sharing my Underfulfilled Overachiever story and offering, in exchange for a cup of coffee, a "practice" coaching session to anyone who could relate. I expected that maybe a few generous friends might humor me. Instead, I was overwhelmed with appointment requests. Those first meetings led to second and then third sessions. Suddenly, I had regular clients, other UFOAs who were also consummate strivers, who'd checked all the boxes, done all the "right" things, and frequently achieved everything they'd set out to do, yet still found themselves deeply dissatisfied, desperately unfulfilled, and increasingly disconnected from themselves, wondering, *Is this all there is?*

Instead of what I'd been learning in my coaching training, though, what was resonating the most was the method from the guide for living that I'd begun to develop. And it actually seemed to be working. Through our sessions, not only were these fellow UFOAs recovering from their Underfulfilled Overachieverness and building lives they loved living, but I was, too.

The Underfulfilled Overachiever Problem

On its surface, the Underfulfilled Overachiever problem appears to be an individual one. But the more clients I coached, the clearer it became just how widespread and entrenched within our culture the problem really is. How could it be that so many of us were living these great-on-paper lives that felt anything but great on the inside? We had done exactly what society had told us to do, but we had received none of the results that we were promised. Why was no one talking about this?! (It was 2014, and few people were talking about it. Thankfully, that's changing.) This was clearly not just a me (or an any-other-individual-person) problem. It was a systemic one and a pretty freaking consequential one at that—consequential for our health, for our economy, for our culture, and for our general aliveness, individually and collectively.

My question—"What am I doing with my life?"—had morphed into "What are *we* doing with our lives?" and then, finally, "What did they tell us to do with our lives?" with the critical addenda of "How the hell do we stop doing it?" and "What do we do instead?"

At the end of the six-month Not-That Experiment, I still had no job, just a trickle of income, and only a vague plan. Yet somehow, inexplicably, I felt clearer than ever about the direction in which my life was heading next, even though my ultimate destination was still uncertain. An odd thing began to happen, so subtle I didn't even notice at first: I stopped caring so much about The Plan or knowing where I'd be in twelve months, let alone in five years. I only cared about how I felt toward what I was doing now.

I was also super pissed. We had been taught to play by the rules of a game that didn't exist anymore and maybe never had. We were sold a story that if we worked hard enough and made the right choices, we would live successful, happy, and fulfilled lives. But what happens when you end up with all the success and none of the fulfillment?

In the decade since, I've heard some version of the same story from thousands of UFOAs: "I did everything I was supposed to do. I worked hard, then even harder, and achieved all the things I set out to achieve. I was showered with praise and admiration and never doubted that if I did all this, I would 'make it' and be happy. But I'm not."

For some, this looked like getting an alphabet's worth of degrees, climbing the corporate ladder, and amassing awards and bonuses. For others, it was getting married by twenty-five, having a bunch of kids by thirty-five, and living in an *Architectural Digest*–worthy home. For still others, it was being the "perfect" daughter and granddaughter, dutifully caring for their elders. Or it was rejecting capitalism and Big Education to live off the grid. It didn't matter what the "supposed to" was. The narrative was always the same.

I've heard this story from C-suite executives of public companies, founders of successful start-ups, tenured professors, law firm partners, bestselling authors, EICs of magazines, valedictorians and veterinarians, restaurateurs and executive chefs, investment bankers and visual artists, heart surgeons and meditation instructors, engineers and educators, college freshmen and PhD candidates, politicians and musicians, people at nonprofits and people in public health, people just out of college and people on their third and fourth careers. I've heard this story across the age spectrum, from sixteen to seventy-four, and from first-generation college graduates to multi-generational legacy Ivy Leaguers to those with no college attendance at all. I've heard this story told all over the world, in cities and sub-urbs and rural areas, on the coasts and in the Midwest and the South, in the United States, Canada, Australia, Germany, South Africa, Italy, France, Norway, the United Kingdom, the Nether-lands, Japan, South America, and more.

This is not a niche problem. UFOAs are everywhere. And our numbers are only growing.

What this means is that you are not alone and you never have to be by yourself with this struggle again. That deep dissatisfaction and painful disconnection from your life and yourself that persist no matter how many accomplishments you have or will accumulate? You're not making those up. That existential chafing and the longing you carry for meaning and purpose that occupies the gaping hole where fulfillment was supposed to be? They are simply classic signs that you, too, are an Underfulfilled Overachiever.

It's also not your fault. There is nothing wrong with you. You haven't screwed anything up. The fact that you're stuck, lost, and confused is not some individual failing. You weren't born believing that you need to achieve your way into fulfillment. You were pro-grammed to think this way. You were taught that if you can just be successful, you'll be happy. You were told that enough of the "right" accomplishments would prove your worth to the world and thus pro-tect you and set you up for all the success in life.

You were taught a lie.

Living in a Destinational World

My hope is that hearing you're not alone or at fault comes as a welcome relief. And yet the fundamental problem remains: you're unfulfilled. As Underfulfilled Overachievers, we see success, broadly speaking, as the organizing principle of our lives. We're not discreet about it, either. We call it by a cute and catchy name: hustle culture! We brag about our intense busyness and our "rise and grind" attitudes. Side hustles are a badge of honor. Going "above and beyond" in our jobs is routine. Our primary purpose, unabashedly, is achievement. This is the Underfulfilled Overachiever problem at its core: we believe that the fulfillment we're looking for is inherently linked to achievement and success.

Most of us UFOAs were shaped around assumptions and expectations of achievement from the very beginning of our lives. Take the classic question that is often posed to children: "What do you want to be when you grow up?" You may have noticed that the response tends to be favorable toward occupations such as doctor, lawyer, and engineer and less favorable toward those with perceived lower earning potential, such as bus driver, fireman, and artist. Why?

Because what is really being asked is "What do you intend to achieve?"—a gauge for how successful and therefore how valuable that child is likely to become.

We praise kids for being "good students," by which we don't mean curious and engaged. We mean the results, the high grades, the awards, the honors. A conscientious student is taught to focus more on grades and test scores than on *what* they are actually learning and retaining. Our whole education system is built on this principle.

This means prioritizing productivity—achievement's codependent partner—above almost all else. The central question at the start of the day becomes "How can I be the most productive today?" In other words, how can I achieve the most? How can I eat, sleep, and move in a way that optimizes my productivity? What's the commute that will allow me to be the most productive in transit? (Hello, Wi-Fi–enabled Google commuter buses!) Clients tell me they go to therapy, meditate, and practice self-care *because it makes them more productive.*

The belief that achievement is the path to a meaningful life is further reinforced by our social institutions. Take, for example, what we call employment "benefits"—health insurance and 401(k) retirement savings accounts—which, by my estimation, should really be called "essentials." By tying these "benefits" to our employment, we tie our very survival in not-so-subtle terms to our accomplishments, such that, generally speaking, the more accomplished we are, the better our health insurance/health care and retirement savings contributions and options become. In the US, at least, more success literally means more insurance.

But if all this is supposed to be for our benefit, to guarantee our security and happiness, why, then, do almost 50 percent of millennials report symptoms of depression and/or anxiety disorders* and 84 percent report symptoms of burnout?† And why are these numbers only continuing to rise, even since the height of the COVID pandemic? Those are not metrics of success by anyone's definition. Those are not the statistics of a fulfilled generation. Clearly, something in our system is very broken, and it's not going away.

Achievement on its own isn't the issue though; the problem is the expectation that with achievement comes fulfillment. This means that we are orienting every aspect of our lives toward that achievement outcome. It's not about the why or the how of the child's becoming; it's about the end result. It's not about the learning or the competency but about the GPA and the perceived prestige of the degree. It's not about the most enjoyable way to get to work or being and feeling well during your day; it's about what each choice can earn you. What these things have in common is that they are all about the *destination*. We Underfulfilled Overachievers don't do all this achievement chasing because it's human nature or because it brings us pleasure. We do it because we've been trained to live Destinationally.

We Are Living Destinationally

Put bluntly, the way we've been taught to "do" life is all wrong.

Destinational Living is the Underfulfilled Overachiever's funda-

---

*Chris Lee, "Latest Federal Data Show That Young People Are More Likely Than Older Adults to Be Experiencing Symptoms of Anxiety or Depression," KFF, March 20, 2023, https://www.kff.org/coronavirus-covid-19/press-release/latest-federal-data-show-that -young-people-are-more-likely-than-older-adults-to-be-experiencing-symptoms-of -anxiety-or-depression/.

†"Workplace Burnout Survey," Deloitte, https://www2.deloitte.com/us/en/pages/about -deloitte/articles/burnout-survey.html.

mental approach to life, by which we pursue tangible, recognizable outcomes based on the lie that these will guarantee our security and happiness. It's an approach that focuses exclusively on a demonstrable end result and disregards whatever happens on the way there. It's an "end justifies the means" philosophy of life. This is the stuff of climbing ladders and linear, predetermined career paths. You must know exactly where you are going in your career and life, and how you will get there, before you can even begin to experience living it. Destinational Living says, "Decide what you want your life to look like, come up with a ten-year plan, and then work backward to determine the most advantageous place from which to start." In the abstract, this is a lovely idea, and one we so badly want to be real. There's a reason why it's the dominant cultural paradigm. It's incredibly comforting to believe that the world and our futures are so reliable and predictable that we can plot it all out in advance—we just have to put our minds to it. How seductive to think that we have the utmost control over the world around us. If only it were true. The problem is that, as it turns out, we cannot reverse engineer our lives, or at least not with any measure of authenticity and fulfillment.

I once worked with an Underfulfilled Overachiever who was struggling to decide whether to accept a new job. She told me that she was generally happy in her current role, so I was curious what was appealing to her about the new position. She thought that she should take it because the new title would be easier to leverage elsewhere later. She believed it would increase her visibility. She intended to be a chief marketing officer within the decade, she told me, and this move would help her get there.

All sounds pretty good, right? So my next question was why, then, would she *not* accept this new job offer? What was her hesitation?

Her response: "Honestly, it sounds like kind of a drag. This role isn't really what I enjoy doing or what I am best at, but how can I turn it down? It's such an objectively great opportunity."

This is textbook Destinational Living. The priority is the destination—chief marketing officer—and getting there as quickly as possible. The focus is definitely not the work itself in the intervening years, not the enjoyment of the work, not even the impact of the work. Who cares if the trip is miserable? It'll be worth it once you "arrive," right?

Wrong.

When we practice Destinational Living, we end up living from accomplishment to accomplishment, from checkbox to checkbox, and rarely realize that's what we're doing. There's a cultural consensus around Destinational Living as the optimal approach to life, and it has become so predominant that we forget it's just *one* way to live, not the only way, much like Kleenex is but one brand of facial tissue and Google is but one search engine.

Destinational Living means outsourcing our decision-making. What is impressive, what is valuable—these are defined not by what matters to us personally but, rather, by what matters to others and which ways of life, which checkboxes, the collective has deemed "worthy." We're incentivized to defer to sources outside ourselves for guidance on what counts, what to do next, by when, and in what order. It takes all the you-ness out of the equation. We, as individuals, barely factor in.

The word *should* is a dead giveaway that Destinational outsourcing is at play. I *should* major in econ, not creative writing. I *should* order the salad, not the pasta. I *should* own a house, go to grad school, be further along in my career, get married, have children, accrue ten thousand followers, and so on. You probably have an abundance of your own "shoulds" coming to mind right now, about which I'd encourage you to ask, "Says who?"

In effect, we're "life plagiarizing," and we don't even realize it. We're essentially taking someone else's life trajectory and imitating it, maybe changing a few words or details along the way. It's attempting to copy something—a life—that is meant to be proprietary. It's asking, "What did that person do to achieve such success?" and then turning around and saying, "Okay, got it. Copy, paste. I'll have what she's having." What the logic of Destinational Living neglects is that success isn't arbitrary or generic; it is deeply personal. One size does not fit all. The lives of the people you admire are meant to be footnotes, parts of your research, but they can't be your whole story.

I spoke to a group of high school students a few years ago, and I asked them, as a demonstration, what they wanted to be when they "grew up." Answers like "architect," "computer scientist," "pediatrician," and "CEO" peppered the room. And then one student gave the most honest answer I've heard to date: "I don't care what I do," she said. "I just want to be successful." Every one of the students' responses was an example of Destinational Living, but this answer exemplified Destinational Living in its purest form, stripped of all artifice.

What, then, are we really talking about when we say "success"? Why did that student aspire to being successful? Why do any of us?

What I've observed is that when we say we want to be successful, what we are actually saying is that we want to *feel* successful. That feeling of success we're looking for? It's called fulfillment. The lie of Destinational Living is its presumption that success and fulfillment are one and the same. What most of us UFOAs eventually learn the hard way is that *being,* or *appearing,* successful (achieving the title of architect, computer scientist, CEO, parent, spouse, or homeowner) is a very different experience than *feeling* successful—that is, from being fulfilled.

Fulfillment is the feeling of being filled up or whole—full of your own particular life, full of your most true self. It's the feeling of being precisely where you are meant to be, even when it is hard or doesn't feel awesome. It's a deep sense of belonging to yourself. When you design a life that is uniquely well suited to you and distinctly your own, you are living in your full integrity. You become the owner of a life that feels like yours.

Colloquially, this is that "best life" we're always reading about. Only it's the version that actually feels the best, as opposed to the one that just looks the best on paper and on social media apps. This kind of fulfillment is not naturally co-occurring with generic on-paper success.

When we imagine being on our deathbeds and looking back on what mattered to us, it's fulfillment we're trying to bring into focus. *Did I do what I came here to do? Did I show up as the truest, most authentic version of myself as often as possible?*

The problem with these questions is that they aren't very useful on a grounded, practical, and experiential day-to-day level. Rather than taking us deeper into ourselves, on their own, they tend to overwhelm us, taking us out of our bodies and out of our lives. What I care about is not just how we think about these big existential, philosophical questions but, more importantly, how we *live* them and apply them to our lives in a genuine, concrete way. This begins with the key fact that what we find fulfilling is unique to each of us. Your fulfillment belongs only to you. It cannot be outsourced.

So much of the big work here is extricating ourselves from Destinational Living, from the norms and rules that have expired or never worked in the first place. That's not easy when the effects of Destinational Living, individually and collectively, are only just now starting to be recognized at scale. Thankfully, there is an increasingly growing consensus around the debilitating brokenness of our achievement- and productivity-obsessed system. If you google "hustle culture" today, you'll see more search results for content outlining its toxicity than for content proselytizing its benefits. There has also been a proliferation of excellent articles and new books on not only burnout but also the future of work as a whole and its place in our lives and culture.

In part, we have technology to thank for this burgeoning awareness. It was the ability to work from anywhere with mobile devices that enabled the culture of "always on" in the first place. Now we've arrived at the inevitable backlash, a collective cry for the off switch. The conversation around work culture was only further catalyzed and then crystallized during the COVID pandemic. A break from routine and social norms forced people to see how truly unfulfilled they are and, perhaps even more importantly, how little safety and security, let alone fulfillment, our cherished achievements have earned us. As with any major loss or life-altering event, it forced us to ask ourselves what really matters to us and why—only in this instance, we asked the question en masse all at once. Hence all the hype about the "Great Resignation," the term given to the predicted trend of large numbers of employees voluntarily resigning from their jobs in the wake of the pandemic, which I think speaks more to the experience of widespread reevaluation of our lives than to an actual collective quitting.

At the same time, hastened by the COVID pandemic, the foundational premise of Destinational Living—the myth of certainty—has been unraveling. Destinational Living assumes that the future is knowable and fixed, or at least reasonably predictable. And yet, suddenly, the supposedly surefire paths to success revealed themselves to be not such sure things after all, and the very destinations to which we were en route suddenly no longer existed, if they ever existed at all. Commercial real estate would always be highly lucrative, they said . . . until we didn't leave our houses or return to offices. Traditional media jobs would always be secure . . . until the internet became widely available. A computer science degree would always be lucrative and in demand . . . until AI came along. The list goes on. It has become increasingly difficult to assume that there is a "there" there, as the saying goes.

Destinational Living necessarily depends on predictability and certainty—a certainty that the past twenty years has destroyed. What was easy to believe in the 1980s and '90s, during a time of relative stability, became a lot harder to accept for millennials, who came of age in a post–9/11 world, who entered the workforce among the rubble of the 2008 financial crisis, and whose prime professional and personal years were effectively ground to a halt by a pandemic.

In other words, to practice Destinational Living, we must believe in our ability to predict the future, which is, of course, naive at best and, at worst, incredibly hubristic. The hard truth is that we've been trading our authenticity for a sense of control and certainty that doesn't exist. Brené Brown, I think, puts it best in her book *The Gifts of Imperfection*. "Caution: If you trade in your authenticity for safety," she warns, "you may experience the following: anxiety, depression, eating disorders, addiction, rage, blame, resentment, and inexplicable grief."

☑ *Anxiety and depression and declining mental health.*

The list doesn't stop there. Let's look at the three other main symptoms of Destinational Living: compulsive achieving, productivity hoarding, and perfection paralysis.

Compulsive Achieving:
"More Accomplishments, More Quickly"

When I met Justine, she had already been a successful-on-paper attorney for a decade and had recently made partner at her firm. Becoming partner provided a momentary reprieve, but the accomplishment did not bring her the sense of pride or satisfaction she had expected. She was just relieved she hadn't failed. And then, immediately after, she got scared. "I was so used to upping the ante, I didn't know where else to go, or to climb," she told me. "I felt so trapped."

Her solution? Find more things to accomplish. She joined a nonprofit's board of directors, and then another board. She taught herself how to code and began building websites as a side hustle. She applied to business school and started working toward an executive MBA on evenings and weekends. She had a business idea and had set her sights on fundraising a round of venture capital investment. She was also barely sleeping and had no time for meaningful relationships. She was now thinking about leaving her law firm, but she'd begun to feel a creeping sense that all she was doing was trying to outachieve her unhappiness. That's when she reached out to me.

This behavior wasn't just limited to her professional life, either. Every part of Justine's life was organized around goals to be accomplished and destinations to be reached. When she traveled to a new city, her goal was to see as many of the top twenty-five attractions as she could, and she strategized extensively to do so as efficiently and effectively as possible. To track her "progress," she maintained a travel spreadsheet that included all the countries in the world and the most purportedly significant cities and locations in each of them.

She refused to go to the same place twice no matter how much she loved it because it was a "waste."

She hosted monthly dinner parties for which she would practice the preparation of a new and "complicated" recipe weeks ahead of time, cooking it again and again until she felt it was perfect. After the party, she would never make that particular dish again. She became a certified sommelier. She ran a marathon, and when we met, she was training for a triathlon.

She recited all these things to me in one sentence, seemingly without taking a breath. I asked her, "Of everything you just mentioned, which of these activities do you truly enjoy?"

She looked stunned. We sat in silence for a few moments. "No one has ever asked me that," she said. "I have no idea . . . Option D? None of the above?"

I followed by asking her why, then, she was doing them. Again, silence. "How could I not know the answer to that question?" she finally said. "Because I have to? It doesn't feel like I have a choice. I know that doesn't make any sense, but that's what it feels like."

This is what we commonly refer to as "overachieving," but I find the term to be a little misleading. It sounds so aspirational! Especially to those who are practicing overachievers. Who wouldn't want to be an overachiever?! "Over" is meant to indicate excessive, but in a world where going above and beyond is glorified, being called an overachiever can sound a lot like a compliment. But I assure you it's not, and here's why.

The overachieving that occurs when we live Destinationally is more akin to *compulsive* achieving. Justine didn't *want* to be accomplishing all these things. None of them were meaningful to her or additive to her life. They were arbitrary boxes to be checked. She was anxiously achieving, not *aligned* achieving. It wasn't just unful-filling to her; it was also beginning to make her miserable, even sick. She'd stopped getting her period, she had eczema for the first time in her life, she couldn't remember the last time she'd slept through the night, and her digestion, well, let's just say it wasn't doing what it was supposed to do. But sometimes that just happens, right?! A co-incidence, surely!

Justine wasn't a masochist, nor was she "crazy." What was driving her was a desire not for the achievement of the goals themselves but for something beyond that—the safety and security and fulfill-ment that she had been led to believe were waiting for her just as soon as she arrived at enough destinations. Justine used the word *trapped* when she described making partner at her law firm. This milestone for which she had worked so hard meant that she had sup-posedly reached the peak of her law career. But instead of elation, she felt anxiety. Where would she find more achievements to accu-mulate now? She needed more gold stars! She couldn't see the next rung on the ladder, which made her feel insecure and vulnerable. So she found new things to achieve and new destinations to shoot for and was successful in reaching them. But none of it made her feel better.

You see, the more you try to achieve in order to acquire safety and happiness, the more unsafe and unhappy you become. The more unsafe and unhappy you feel, the more you will try to achieve. Wash, rinse, repeat. The irony is that the overachievement is what drives the underfulfillment. It makes it worse, not better. In other words, what we UFOAs think of as the cure is really the poison.

As long as you're living Destinationally, achievement is a defense mechanism, a default response to insecurity. It comes from fear, not from an aligned and organic desire. It's defensive, not expansive, creative, or inspired. I have hard news, my fellow UFOAs: achievement will not keep you safe, nor will it guarantee you a happy life.

Are You a Compulsive Achiever?

Think of a big goal on which you're currently focusing—professional or educational may be best for this exercise, but any is fine (including a past achievement, if you prefer).
Then, like I asked Justine, ask yourself:

- What is my "why" for this goal?

- Why is doing this thing important to me?

- What do I think I will get from it once I achieve it—security, happiness, and/or fulfillment?

- Do I truly enjoy it?

- Do I actually *want* to work toward this thing?

Productivity Hoarding: "Always Be Doing"

Most Underfulfilled Overachievers also have what journalist Anne Helen Petersen once called a "broken productivity brain." Productivity hoarding—a preoccupation with being productive at all times and at all costs—is another common symptom of living Destinationally and is usually found sprinting hand in hand with its older sibling, compulsive achieving. Productivity hoarding, sometimes called toxic productivity or "overfunctioning," follows a similar psychological logic as compulsive achieving, but it's focused on task completion as opposed to goal completion. It's a miniversion of compulsive achievement that shows up in your day-to-day instead of over the course of a decade, a career, or a life. The daily to-do list is to productivity hoarding what the five-year plan is to compulsive achievement. Productivity hoarding, in other words, is incremental overachieving. Its catchphrase would be something like "Always be doing."

Remember all the banana bread and sourdough starters and calls to learn a new language at the beginning of the COVID pandemic? Hello, productivity hoarding! At a time of extreme uncertainty and true risk to our lives, we turned to productivity hoarding because it gave us a sense of control and agency in the face of powerlessness. It was a way of self-soothing. *The more productive we are, the safer and more fulfilled we will be!* And then: *Since we can't clearly see ways to be productive, we'll just start making "productive" stuff up!*

As with achieving, the point here is not that productivity is "bad," and it is certainly not the case that all productivity is productivity hoarding. The question is whether it's *programmed* productivity or what I'll call *pure* productivity. The former comes from the Destinational belief that more doing means more worth and more safety. The latter comes from a genuine and aligned desire, a concept we'll get to in the coming chapters.

For one of our early sessions, Justine arrived frantic, full of apologies for showing up four minutes behind schedule. The reason she was late, she explained, was because of an extra-credit assignment she was working on for her executive MBA program. She also said it was a silly assignment that was a waste of time. When I asked her why, then, she was doing it, she told me it hadn't occurred to her not to. As with most UFOAs, it was default behavior, not a conscious choice: "Because you *should* always do the extra credit. It's the right, conscientious thing to do. And you wouldn't want to give the professor the impression that you're not committed! You need that A+."

For the work that Justine and I were doing, this was a perfect "teachable moment" to explain what I suspected was really going on. Destinational Living tells an Underfulfilled Overachiever who is (always) feeling scared and uncertain about her future, "YES! Another opportunity for me to be productive and demonstrate my worth and earn more safety! Surely this will protect me from future pain." A UFOA will do whatever it takes to get that assignment done, regardless of what the task is, her capacity, her level of interest, or even the fact that she's already earning an A+ in the class.

I suggested to Justine that the assignment didn't have to be an automatic yes. She had some choice in the matter; she could decide to do the extra-credit work, but she could also decide not to. What if her decision to do it or not to do it was based on the assignment itself and whether it resonated with her as personally meaningful and constructive learning rather than based on what it would get her or what it would protect her from? For UFOAs, any productivity is "good" productivity. But I want to stress that this is not the case. Productivity is only useful when it's pure productivity—when it's aligned for *you*.

Honestly? I'm still deprogramming this one, too. It was years after I had stopped productivity chasing, or at least stopped believing that it was an effective tool, when one night I noticed myself reciting every "productive" thing I'd done that day, as if I were counting sheep: "Responded to Jane's email, had three client sessions, paid that doctor's invoice, prepared a healthful and delicious dinner, called my mom, bought flowers, finished the novel I was reading, went on a walk with Abigail, interviewed a new admin . . ." I'd never noticed myself doing that before. What was that?!

Thinking back, I realized that from the time I was really young, I'd always soothed my anxious mind at bedtime and put myself to sleep by listing all the ways in which I'd been productive that day. No one told me to do this, and I didn't understand what I was doing or why it worked. I'd stumbled upon my own personal antidote to anxiety: productivity affirmations. Monsters under the bed? How many math problems had I done, how many books had I read, how many goals had I scored, how many laps had I run? Feeling lonely? How many times had I spoken up in class, how many times had I been helpful to a classmate, how many dances had I choreographed in the living room with my sister? Worried about a sick grandparent? How many puzzles had I done, how many new vocab words had I memorized, how many pieces of broccoli had I eaten at dinner?

For as long as I could remember, I had been affirming my productivity as an attempt to affirm my safety and my worth. You can't really get any more UFOA (or child of late-stage capitalism) than that!

Are You a Productivity Hoarder?

- Look at your current to-do list and notice how you feel when you look at these tasks.

  - Do you feel:

    a. Inspired and energized? (Pure productivity)

    b. Or, disinterested and full of dread? (Programmed productivity)

  - How many things on this list reflect programmed productivity (shoulds) versus pure productivity (wants)?

- Do you wear "productivity" like a badge of honor?

- Do you consider being "productive" good and something to be proud of versus "unproductive" bad and/or something to feel guilty about?

- The next time you feel anxious or insecure, notice what you're inclined to do to "fix" the feeling. Is it to do something "productive"?

Perfection Paralysis: "Get It Right"

During the eight years I worked for Google, I almost left twice with a hard-and-fast plan. The first time, I went so far as to be flown out for a series of interviews at a publishing start-up. I got wined and dined and was given an extremely competitive offer. I even verbally *accepted* the position and received the contract. All that was left to do was sign and return it. And that's when I freaked out. Was this the "right" decision? What if it was the "wrong" one? I polled everyone I knew, but there was no consensus. Some said it was a "strategic" move and great for my career, while others said it was a self-imposed demotion. Some thought the start-up was a "unicorn," and others thought it was a dud. I needed someone to tell me what the right, perfect, and uncriticizable choice was. A pros-and-cons list wasn't going to save me, but I made ten of them anyway, willing some new thought to come in and tip the balance. I barely slept. I called in sick to work. I agonized. I made excuses for the delay. I asked for more time. I let the decision bleed into Christmas and that end-of-December no-man's-land before the New Year and ruined the festivities for everyone around me; I sleepwalked through the holidays, alternating between complete disengagement and uncontrollable tears. And then I just . . . didn't sign it. I rescinded my acceptance.

The second time I almost left, I decided I wanted to take a sabbatical to go work abroad with a women's microfinance organization. I was fascinated by the topic and by the organization, and for months I eagerly researched late into the night—totally abandoning my previous disengaged norm of *The Real Housewives*, *Grey's Anatomy*, and Seamless delivery. I didn't know where it might lead or what it might "get" me. I had no outcome in mind. For a brief moment, I wasn't thinking Destinationally or outsourcing my decision-making; it was a "want" instead of a "should."

When I finally got up enough courage to talk to the director of my team about it and request a leave, he talked me out of it in five minutes flat. I had all the conviction in the world as I walked in with my plan, but I walked out of that meeting as if my plan had never existed. All it took was one dissenting opinion sowing a few seeds of doubt and fear for me to abandon my idea altogether.

The meeting with the director, whom we'll call Dan, was over video. Dan was in his office in New York City, and I was in a conference room in San Francisco called Presidio Heights (all the conference rooms were named after local neighborhoods). It was a boardroom-style conference room, which, though unintentional and selected because it was the only space available—gave the meeting a level of gravitas that felt oddly congruent with how weighty this decision felt to me. Dan was at his desk in his glass-walled office when he appeared on the gigantic floor-to-ceiling video. The surround-sound speaker system boomed as he spoke, his giant face filling the screen. The effect was that of some supreme and omniscient authority lording over me.

He kicked off the meeting by smirking and saying, "So, I heard you want to make a really dumb choice." Though he tried to pass it off as a joke, it was obvious that it was not, in fact, a joke. This tactic—"I'm going to pretend this is a joke so that you can't call me out, but we both know I am actually quite serious"—was common (and commonly pissed me off).

Dan told me that I should definitely not walk away from the best company in the world. He reminded me to think *logically* and *strategically* and to understand how this would sabotage my career. He said the team would evolve without me and I'd have nothing to come back to. He said I'd look flaky and unfocused. My future bosses would question my loyalty and commitment to my team, and my colleagues would lose trust in me. He warned me that I didn't want to forfeit such an incredibly powerful network. He told me not to be frivolous with my career and asked how such a choice would in any way shape or help my professional prospects. He told me that unless I was certain this new field was the one I really wanted to be in for the rest of my life, I shouldn't waste my time.

For the grand finale, he explained that this was simply not a wise move and that I was too smart for such a thing. He also threw in some bonus flattery about how brilliant and talented I was, how he wanted me on his team, and how he intended to invest in me and my future. The very last thing he said, which would for *years* after reverberate in my mind anytime I thought about making any kind of change, was "Don't be stupid."

Perhaps there are scenarios where this would be decent advice and not just an intimidation tactic to preserve the head count. Sometimes you need a good friend to point out your blind spots. But he wasn't my friend, and I wasn't asking for advice. And this "advice"— if we can call it that—was for his benefit, not mine.

For a long time, I was perplexed and ashamed about both of these near-quitting situations. How mortifying that I could be so easily dissuaded from something about which I had such assuredness! What did this say about me? How had that happened?! I'm still mortified that as someone who takes pride in being conscientious and consistent, I was unprofessional enough to accept and then unaccept a job. Such was the depth of my confusion and UFOA sickness. (And yes, for those of you out there wondering, I've seriously considered strategically not including this embarrassing story here as a result!)

Destinational Living conditions us to achieve more, to achieve more quickly (compulsive achieving), and to therefore always be doing (productivity hoarding). But all of that counts only if we do it "right," according to the court of public opinion. We have this idea, consciously or not, that there is a single, objectively correct choice to be made. Each decision feels like a test.

I became so consumed with making the "right" decision that I couldn't make any decision at all. I became completely paralyzed because I was so terrified of getting kicked off Success Island with one "incorrect," not-unanimously-approved-by-every-person-I-could-ever-come-across decision and losing all that promised security and happiness toward which I'd been working for so long.

This understandable fixation with not only achieving success but also achieving correctly and properly—perfectly—is a form of perfectionism. The very belief that there *is* an objectively right way to do things is perfectionist. Perfectionism has great PR and is often conflated with the pursuit of excellence—so virtuous! But perfectionism has nothing to do with doing a good job. Perfection preoccupation has much more to do with conformity and belonging and much less to do with actual performance. My favorite definition of UFOA perfectionism is being "beyond reproach"—being uncriticizable and unjudgable. UFOA perfectionism is not so much about being perfect as it is about *appearing* perfect.

When I was deciding whether to accept that start-up job offer and then, later, whether to take the sabbatical and work abroad, I thought that I needed to build complete and total consensus. I suffered because I couldn't be certain that my decision would be met with unanimous approval, and I feared appearing "imperfect" in someone's, anyone's, eyes. Such a risk was so intolerable to my Destinational sensibilities that I instead chose to stay where I was: stuck. This kind of decision paralysis is where UFOA perfectionism usually leads.

The promise of perfectionism is the "right" kind of success, the best and winningest of achievements that will earn us the greatest amount of fulfillment: a.k.a. The Perfect Life™. Sounds great, right? The problem is that, in practice, it doesn't create progress; it only creates paralysis. What we UFOAs are doing to try to keep ourselves safe and "beyond reproach" ends up just keeping us stuck. Perfectionism does not feel good. There's nothing glam or virtuous about it.

That's the thing about perfectionism—it virtually guarantees the exact situation we're trying to avoid. Focusing on getting the outcome exactly right in the court of public opinion often means getting it wrong for ourselves, or not doing it at all. In other words, perfectionism is just a fancy and socially sanctioned way by which we sabotage ourselves. It's self-sabotage disguised as the pursuit of excellence. It doesn't yield great results, as we're taught to believe—it creates the *same* results; it doesn't create excellence—it creates conformity.

When Dan said, "Don't be stupid," what he was really saying was: *Don't forget that success—accumulating approved achievements— is your primary purpose. Don't do anything to threaten your success and your ability to create the perfect [read: perfect-looking] life.*

"Stupid" would be to choose a nonuniversally approved destination and leave myself vulnerable to judgment and disapproval. By invoking my fear of being unsuccessful and therefore imperfect, he steered me back into the old default of Destinational Living. And I even thanked him for his support and encouragement at the end of our meeting! I felt grateful that he'd "saved" me from the brink of destruction by imperfection.

But Dan isn't the villain here (even though he was kind of an asshole). He was just as much a victim of the same programming that you and I have received. I believe he really thought he was giving me good, sound advice. Advice that also happened to benefit him—he didn't want to deal with head count disruption. Still, it was what he would have done, and it was, in fact, exactly what he had chosen.

It would be years before I'd risk being that "stupid" again.

Do You Have Perfection Paralysis?

Think of a life or career decision that paralyzed you or over which you agonized.

- Were you concerned about making the "correct" or "perfect" decision?

- If so, the "correct" decision according to whom?

- Was the "correct" decision defined as:

  a. The one that you desired the most? (Not perfection paralysis)

  b. Or, the decision that would be "beyond reproach"? (Perfection paralysis)

Two More Markers of Destinational Living: The F-ache and Impostor Syndrome

"Everything you're saying makes sense, but *why* does it all hurt so damn much?!" a client once lamented.

Ah, the Fulfillment Ache. Most of us don't change until we are in enough pain. If you reach out to me, if you pick up this book, it's probably because you're experiencing some level of suffering. Whether it's at the level of an acute breakdown or just around the edges, you know that something isn't working and that you do not feel good. You know that you "should" be happy, but you're not. You feel lost and confused and ashamed because you did everything right, you hit all your marks, and yet here you are, wondering how you got it so wrong. Here you are, standing in the middle of your great-on-paper life, feeling disconnected from your work and your relationships, not to mention from yourself, alternating between wondering whose life you're living and attempting to convince yourself that this is just what it means to be an adult.

The Fulfillment Ache is an existential chafing that develops when there is an alignment gap, when the distance between who we are and what we truly want and the life we are living grows too great for too long. While this intense ache is usually the first symptom we notice, it's actually one of the later symptoms of Destinational Living to emerge, long after we've started compulsively achieving and productivity hoarding and become paralyzed with perfection. The ache is the result of these symptomatic UFOA behaviors eroding alignment over time: compulsive, blind achieving instead of aligned achieving, programmed productivity instead of pure productivity, and perfection paralysis instead of Directional progress. Every achievement, every

41

item checked off the programmed-productivity checklist, and every moment of imperfection staved off only deepen the chasm and enhance the fulfillment achiness.

I was never meant to be a Google tech exec in an open-layout office space thinking about sales and deals and the latest in mobile consumer technology, because I'm meant to be doing this right here, writing and coaching and teaching and thinking about life design and how to live a meaningful life. There was a massive alignment gap, and it's there where my F-ache developed. It's not that the former was "bad" and the latter is "good." Rather, it's like I was handed a script and was just doing my best to play my role well enough that the show could go on. I was performing in someone else's play, faking it in hopes of making it.

In fact, that's why I refer to the Fulfillment Ache as the F-ache—yes, pronounced like *fake*—because that's ultimately what we UFOAs are doing: faking it, trying to achieve our way into happiness, cosplaying success, and inhabiting not only lives that don't belong to us but also lives that we didn't even want in the first place. Not because they're shitty lives, but because they're not ours.

Back in 2016, I heard the poet David Whyte beautifully describe this F-acheful phenomenon in an interview with Krista Tippett on her podcast, *On Being*:

> *One of the interesting qualities of being human is . . . we're the only part of creation that can actually refuse to be ourselves. . . . We can get afraid of the way we are, and we can temporarily put a mask over our face and pretend to be somebody else or something else. And the interesting thing is, then we can take it another step of virtuosity and forget that we were pretending to be someone else and become the person we were . . . just pretending to be in the first place.*

That's the F-ache-causing UFOA condition in a nutshell. Of course it hurts. Performing is an exhausting, full-time job. Masks are heavy. Hiding from who you are is excruciating.

The F-ache is a consequence of this "faking" and masking, a symptom of the Destinational Living model. It's not the problem itself, but it does serve a purpose. It hurts, sometimes unbearably, precisely so that you realize its source—the act of faking it, the state of being out of alignment with yourself and your life—and you stop ignoring it. Because it's not going to go away on its own.

IMPOSTOR SYNDROME

I'd be remiss if I didn't also mention in this context the highly popularized phenomenon of impostor syndrome, since I'd estimate that upward of 90 percent of my clients report experiencing it and list it as one of their top reasons for seeking coaching. Only, impostor syndrome isn't what you think it is.

The term *impostor syndrome*, as it's traditionally defined, refers to the feelings of inadequacy that persist despite evident success and the subsequent fear of being found out. Basically, you feel like you're a phony and a fraud, and you're terrified of being exposed. It's suggested that this is an inaccurate self-belief that can be addressed with "mindset work" and the shifting of "limiting beliefs."

Feelings of impostorhood are a very real thing for UFOAs, but in my experience, they don't stem from a misperception of ourselves and our capabilities. We are convinced that we're impostors not because of some kind of personal competence dysmorphia but because of the larger systems at play. This was first highlighted by Ruchika Tulshyan and Jodi-Ann Burey, who argued that work culture and professional environments were never designed for women, especially women of color, in the first place; they were designed to exclude. So *of course* anyone who's part of an underrepresented group feels like an impostor; there's a big "Keep Out" sign on the door. It's not you, it's them—or "the system."

And this is certainly a large part of it. But another systemic factor is the Destinationalism that's endemic to our work culture and to which we UFOAs subscribe. We feel like impostors because we are behaving like impostors in our own lives. We *are* faking it, so it makes perfect sense that we feel like impostors. That's a wholly accurate feeling to have in response to the pretending we're doing. I absolutely felt like an impostor in my Google life—not because I was secretly bad at my job or incapable of doing it but, rather, because I was posing as a person who wanted to be there, spending my days doing this work, who was passionate about "this space," and who was committed to my "growth" in my role and at the company. I wasn't just trying to convince others, either; I was expending enormous amounts of energy and resources trying to convince myself, too. In this way, impostor syndrome is just another expression of the F-ache, another symptom of being a UFOA living Destinationally. It's there for a reason: to warn us not to permanently become, as Whyte said, "the person we were . . . just pretending to be in the first place."

A New Way

So what's an Underfulfilled Overachiever to do?

Many UFOAs initially misdiagnose their problem as excessive intensity, unreasonable expectations, or perhaps workaholism, assuming that they just have to "care less" about work and realize that "a job is just a job." In 2022, "quiet quitting"—doing the bare minimum required to keep a job but nothing more—dominated headlines, further validating how desperately we're looking for a large-scale mindset shift around how we relate to work. While I support the anti-exploitation sentiment, I'm not a fan of any life strategy that is based on engaging less with your life and yourself, which is how most UFOAs I encounter experience this approach. I'm pretty sure that is not the recipe for fulfillment.

There are also proponents of rejecting the system, disavowing success and achievement, and opting out altogether. There is a movement among young people in China called tangping, or "lying flat"—that is, "a way of life [that includes] not getting married, not having children, not buying a house or a car, and refusing to work extra hours or hold a job at all."* I applaud anyone investigating alternative strategies. And I'm sure there are some for whom lying flat works. But for us UFOAs, ambition is a genuine and earnest part of who we are. Eliminating ambition isn't the path to fulfillment, either. Not to mention that living antithetically to the cultural system is still defining your life in opposition to something, still living defensively *against* instead of *for* something!

This book isn't *Lean In* or *Lie Flat* but a brand-new paradigm for fulfillment that asks (and answers!), "What does a truly fulfilling life look like, and how do we find it?" We've all seen the clichéd advice that "Life is a journey, not a destination" on a motivational poster in the guidance counselor's office or a greeting card in the stationery store. And perhaps we have a sense there's probably some wisdom there. But does anyone actually know how one "journeys"?

---

*Lily Kuo, "Young Chinese Take a Stand Against Pressures of Modern Life—by Lying Down," *Washington Post*, June 5, 2021.

If you were to live life as a journey, what exactly would that entail? Why is a journey better than a destination? Is it? How do you know what direction to journey? Most importantly, why does it matter? Together, we will answer these questions.

We've now established that what we have been doing— Destinational Living—is failing us, badly. But, it does not have to be like this. There's another way. There's a new model available for finding fulfilling success, and it's called Directional Living.

Directional Living is both a philosophy for living and a framework that can be applied to your daily life, no matter where you're starting. This is not a collection of vague concepts and inspirational quotes, nor is it a bunch of "life hacks" and assorted tasks to add to your self-improvement to-do list. It's a radical, deeply transformative approach that will fundamentally challenge everything you've been taught about how to "do" life. There is no single right way to design your life, of course, but this book outlines the most consistently effective tried-and-tested approach that I've found for myself and for my Underfulfilled Overachiever clients. Drawing on insights from a variety of disciplines and traditions—science, psychology, philosophy, various wisdom traditions and spiritual practices—as well as ten years of my own research and observation, what I've discovered, to my initial skepticism and great delight, is that there is, in fact, a universal path to fulfillment, one that yields infinitely varied trajectories and results particular to each of us. This path to fulfillment, Directional Living, will be the focus of the rest of this book.

Here's the catch, Underfulfilled Overachiever: I can't find fulfillment for you. No one can. The good news is that it's all up to you! Not one person in the whole world has more or better answers for you than you. Alleluia! The bad news is also that it's all up to you.

There's not any person in the world to whom you can delegate your life, even when it feels like all you want is for someone to just tell you what to do in order to be happy. This does not mean you are without support or tools. I'm here today handing you your user's guide and operating manual. The five phases of the Underfulfilled Overachiever's path to fulfillment—Recognize, Align, Release, Orient, Iterate—form the backbone of this book. Through these, I'll show you exactly how to make the shift from Destinational to Directional Living in your life.

And while Directional Living often feels the most immediately transferable to careers and our work in the world, it applies equally to romantic partnerships and friendships, to parenting and family relationships, to finances and making a home, to inspiration and creativity, even to what you have for dinner.

Still, this is a book you need to *do* as much as it is one you need to read (or listen to). If you commit to doing this book, you will absolutely finish on a different level of fulfillment, clarity, and ease than where you started. It's not an easy process, and sometimes (always?) it gets worse before it gets better, but it's certainly easier than the alternative suffering of merely surviving, never thriving.

This book itself is a direction, not a destination. My intention is that it's not something you skim through once and never look at again; it's not a "set it and forget it" but a guide that will grow with you and that you will keep handy on your shelf so you can return to it whenever you feel you need it.

Many of the underlying ideas here are not new. Some have been around for centuries. I've done my best to credit sources when they're available, but many of these concepts don't have a specific source. If you feel like you recognize an idea from somewhere else, you probably do. What I offer is a synthesis and an interpretation of many concepts that originated way before me, integrated into a new language that I've found speaks uniquely to Underfulfilled Overachievers at this moment in time. I can assure you that you will never think about achievement or "success" in the same way again.

The closest thing I have to a personal motto is a quotation that's widely attributed to Carl Jung but that, as it turns out, he never actually said at all. It's powerful nevertheless. As the quote goes, "The privilege of a lifetime is to become who you truly are." My greatest hope for you, Underfulfilled Overachiever, is that you get to live fully in this privilege, and my greatest hope for this book is that it can be the guide that shows you how.

Directional Living:
A New Way Forward

In September 2016, right before *that* US presidential election, I held my first group coaching workshop for Underfulfilled Overachievers. It was called WTF Am I Doing with My Life? How to Get Unstuck in Your Career.

I'd recently met Claire Wasserman, who was in the very early stages of launching her new career network for women, Ladies Get Paid. She was putting on a series of town halls and conferences and asked me to teach one of their first seminars. I was hesitant because I'd never done a workshop on this material, but Claire insisted. "All you have to do is the workshop part," she said. "I'll get the people and do the logistics and the everything-else part." It was a pretty compelling offer. I didn't know what, if anything, would come of this event, but I was beginning to realize that I didn't need to know where it would lead, if anywhere. I only needed to know that I couldn't stop thinking about it. So I agreed.

On the day of the workshop, fourteen of us gathered around a great big long table. I sat at one end; Claire sat at the other. The energy in the room was a mix of hope—"What if this actually works? What if I don't have to be miserable anymore?"—and skepticism— "No way this random woman can help me out of this deep, dark hole I've found myself in. I've tried everything and nothing has worked." I welcomed both.

I opened by sharing my own Underfulfilled Overachiever story: the great-on-paper life that felt far, far from great on the inside. Around the table, heads nodded. They were listening intently—not because the story was completely unique to me but precisely because it wasn't. It was their story, too.

Now it was their turn to share. There were freelance producers and creative directors, some advertising execs and brand marketers, a director at a nonprofit. Someone made a twelve-step program joke: "Hi, I'm Saya, and I'm an Underfulfilled Overachiever." Everyone laughed, but it wasn't far from the truth. We were embarking on a form of recovery together.

One after another, each woman told some version of the same story about checking all the boxes and doing all the "right" things only to be unhappy and left wondering, *Is this really all there is?* Each was looking for purpose and meaning and fulfillment while also asking, *Who am I to want Something Bigger, to want to be fulfilled by my work, and to want to feel alive in my own life?*

All of these women were there to find out the secret to getting unstuck. They were there to find their Something Bigger. And they all knew that wasn't what they were doing now, no matter what it was or how good it looked. Sharing and listening to one another that day, these women began to realize that other impressive, intelligent, passionate, creative, driven women were having strikingly similar experiences. Maybe their confusion and disillusionment did not, in fact, mean that they were incompetent. Maybe they weren't to blame after all. Maybe, whatever the problem was, it wasn't theirs to solve on their own. Maybe they weren't alone.

The way forward, I told them, the way to find lasting fulfillment and their Something Bigger, was to stop living *Destinationally*—that is, divesting from the belief that achievement is the path to fulfillment and that your "best life" is a destination waiting for you at the end of that sacred ten-year plan—and start living *Directionally*, where the focus is on moving iteratively in our own personal right direction without needing to know the precise destination. We get unstuck by swapping the question "Where do I need to end up?" for a much simpler one: "Is this single next step Directionally right?"

Directional Living can look as simple as deciding to take a constitutional law class because it feels interesting (direction). Destinational Living, on the other hand, would be starting law school, immediately deciding that your definition of "success" is to be appointed to the Supreme Court one day, and then dedicating every decision you make thereafter to that sole pursuit (destination). Living Directionally means that instead of trying, right out of college, to lock in the company and career from which you'd like to retire at sixty-five (destination), you simply select the next job role you'd like to experience now (direction). Instead of trying to determine whether your date is The One (destination), you focus only on whether you want to go on a second date with them (direction). In fact, you stop trying to decide whether *anything* is The One—the house, the career, the crush, the business, the best friend. You instead decide only on your single next step.

Directional Living looks a lot like the "launch and iterate" approach used across the tech industry. You don't launch a new product with the expectation that it's the final version and that you're going to "set it and forget it." You launch with the minimum viable product (MVP)—the best you can build with what you know today—and you expect to continue iterating as you go. That's why our phones and devices are constantly pushing updates. The goal is not to get it "right" or perfect on the first try or even, necessarily, to adhere to the original plan at all. Rather, the idea is to evolve and fine-tune over time by being alert and responsive to the changing needs and desires of users and markets. The only way to fail is to refuse to iterate and adjust. We've been stuck in an expired "set it and forget it" mentality. We instead want to begin to take the launch-and-iterate approach to life.

A perfect analogy for Directional Living comes from the late novelist E. L. Doctorow:

Writing a novel is like driving a car at night. You can see only as far as your headlights, but you can make the whole trip that way.

Living Directionally is also like driving a car at night. You can't see further than what is illuminated directly in front of you (the next job, date, client, project, twenty-four hours), but you can make the whole trip of your life this way. Your job is just to follow the directions of the GPS—your own personal Inner Navigation System, or INS, which we'll talk much more about—as they appear and to determine what is *Directionally* right. As Anne Lamott suggests in her book on writing, *Bird by Bird*, "This [Doctorow quotation] is right up there with the best advice on writing, or life, I have ever heard."

We think we need a perfectly plotted itinerary and a fully baked master plan when all we need is a direction. I had no idea that my life was going to lead me to coaching. There was no way I could have known this. And, most importantly, I did not *need* to know it! My Inner Navigation System directed me to a coaching class. That was as far as my headlights illuminated. It was more than enough and far from just aimless wandering. Today, I still don't know exactly how my life is going to continue to unfold. I have no ten-year plan, but again, I don't need to have one, because my headlights are spotlighting my next client, course, interview, or article—and that's more than enough to keep me on the road.

Do you feel the freedom in this?! *You don't have to know where you are going.* In fact, you *can't* know where you are going without adopting some willful ignorance about the uncertainty and unpredictability of the unfolding of your life. I would argue that it's even preferable not to know! You're off the hook for figuring out that whole "life purpose" destination and can simply follow the "headlights" of your curiosity and joy instead.

In Directional Living, we work forward, not backward. We are released from the exhausting effort of predicting the future and allowed to instead embrace the evolving and unpredictable world in which we actually live. We shift our mental center of gravity from some vague future finish line to the present task at hand. Instead of asking, "What outcome will this get me?" we ask, "Is this *Directionally* right?" We go from being outcome-oriented to process-oriented. Directional Living shows us that the process—the why and the how on the way to the achievement—matters more for fulfillment than the outcome, the achievement, itself. Directional Living replaces external *compliance* with inner *alignment.* We stop outsourcing our life navigation and start insourcing it. In doing so, we begin to build not generic lives but lives that are particularly and exclusively our own.

Imagine taking a road trip. With a Destinational approach, you would, of course, start with a predetermined destination. You would create—or download—a comprehensive and detailed itinerary. And you'd follow the directions precisely, one after another, all the way to your destination.

I asked the workshop participants for Destinational examples from their own lives, and Jane, an executive director at a nonprofit organization, raised her hand. Jane couldn't remember a time when she didn't have that precise career destination in mind. She shared that both of her parents were also executive directors at nonprofits; she felt strongly that it was the most valuable and impactful career one could have. They had advised her about what undergrad and master's programs to enroll in, what internships to take, and what early jobs to seek out so that she could achieve this career as soon as possible. Her role had simply been to handle the logistics and execution.

Jane had been on a Destinational road trip her entire life. Her parents had handed her the itinerary for her life, and she had dutifully followed it to a T. She had made her life choices based solely on the place she'd planned to end up. Each step along the way was only valuable insofar as it was a leg on the travel schedule, advancing her to that end goal.

Now contrast this with a Directional road trip. Instead of speeding your way to that final destination, you determine what *direction* feels most compelling, and you set out, relying on your Inner Navigation System to guide you as you go. You know that your INS will make the necessary adjustments in real time and that you can reroute, make spontaneous pit stops, make wrong turns, and even change directions without jeopardizing your ability to arrive safely— because that's what navigation systems are for! You make your way by simply deciding at each juncture what the next leg of your trip will be. You don't try to see anything beyond what the shining "headlights" of your interest show you.

In this *Directional* approach, you are creating the itinerary in real time, you are an active participant in your trip, and you are responsive to your internally and externally changing environments. You get to engage in the moment with your changing desires and moods, the weather, the road conditions. There is more uncertainty at the beginning, sure, but the result becomes infinitely more inspired, innovative, engaging, organic, and authentic. The result, whatever it is, however it evolves, will be uniquely well suited to you. It will be *yours*.

So how do you start? You start with a Directional idea and a willingness to pay attention to what your headlights reveal—to what feels compelling at this moment in time, no matter how dark it is beyond that. The darkness is of no matter, so long as your headlights are turned on, securely illuminating what is directly in front of you. All you have to do is keep going. Admittedly, this may feel dangerous for UFOAs. But just as a sixteen-year-old with a permit learns to drive safely in the dark with practice, we, too, with practice, become comfortable enough to maneuver this way.

What might your headlights be showing you right now?

Here are some other ways of asking this question: What lights you up? When was the last time you felt fully alive? What do you most look forward to doing? What do you do "just because"? In the professional realm, specifically, has there ever been another career or type of work that you fantasized about but dismissed for one reason or another?

In the workshop, I came back to Jane, and she knew her answer to these questions instantly: "Photography." But almost before she'd gotten it out of her mouth, before I or anyone else could react, she shot it down as a path for consideration. Photography was not a career, she said; rather, it was just a hobby. She insisted that she wouldn't be able to support herself financially.

Let's dig into this a bit. Were Jane's assumptions about a career in photography accurate? Maybe and maybe not. The point is that she didn't need to know yet. She couldn't know. Instead, once again, think of driving at night: just the headlights. If we play out this photography scenario as a Directional road trip, Jane could begin by simply perusing the course catalog of a university photography program. Her only job would be to do an internet search for some local photography schools, like the School of Visual Arts in New York City, and browse to see what, if anything, jumped out at her—to see what felt Directionally right for the next single step.

Maybe she finds a one-day Saturday workshop—super-low stakes. She signs up. She loves it, and she loves the professor, and that professor is about to teach a semester-long course on portraits, so she enrolls in that, not because she needs it to lead somewhere but simply because it feels Directionally right. Maybe she then becomes a teaching assistant for this very course so that she can take more classes for free, and she discovers that what she really loves is *teaching* photography and that she's incredibly talented at it. Maybe she becomes a professor of photographic arts. And then she starts a podcast on photography, sponsored by the school, in which she talks about the creative process with other photographers and visual artists.

Or maybe the idea that really lights her up after taking a photography course is pitching her nonprofit colleagues on an exhibit displaying portraits of the people whose lives the organization has impacted, along with a fundraiser and an awareness campaign. Maybe it gets featured in *Time Out* magazine and she suddenly has an influx of demand for her private photography services. Or maybe, after seeing the success of the photography campaign, she decides to become a consultant for other nonprofits, helping them use visual art and photography to elevate their impact.

Or maybe photography remains something that she does just for herself, something that reminds her of who she is, something that feels distinctly *hers*, making it easier for her to recognize that the nonprofit side of raising money and awareness for an Alzheimer's cure is just *not* Directionally right. But you know what does feel Directionally right to her? The research side of finding a cure for Alzheimer's. And so maybe she starts working in a research lab. She gets another degree . . . Who knows? Her mandate is simply to follow the single next Directionally right step.

Why is this approach better than Destinational Living? Because we simply cannot know which of these scenarios will transpire— and the actual scenario will most likely be something else that's bigger and even better than we could possibly imagine. Jane has no way of knowing (or controlling, despite her best efforts) whether she'll hit it off with the teacher, whether she'll get some press, or what aspect of photography she'll even like, if any.

Our capacity to imagine destinations for ourselves is severely limited by the fact that we *can't predict the future*. If you insist on defining the final destination as, say, becoming a famous gallery photographer or even just becoming a photographer who makes a living from your art, you absolutely might get there, but more likely than not, you'll end up feeling like a failure because you picked an arbitrary and extremely narrow destination that was never meant for you. And if you do get there, it's very likely that you'll be confronted by what Dr. Tal Ben-Shahar has called the "arrival fallacy"— when you arrive, the destination won't feel like what you thought it would, and you'll find yourself disillusioned, stuck, and still longing for fulfillment, even though you've achieved everything you set out to achieve.

This is the biggest thing we miss out on with the Destinational approach: responsiveness to our real and ever-changing environments—external *and* internal. Hell-bent on that one destination, we move through life on autopilot. We're not even really doing the steering, just keeping our foot heavy on the gas. When we stop needing to predict exactly where we are going, opportunities emerge. New options that were once inconceivable to us present themselves when we interact with the world as it is, as opposed to how we anticipate it will be.

This is why, in Directional Living, we work forward, not backward. We need to *live into* the questions "What is this life about?" and "What is my Something Bigger?" We can't just sit at our desks with our spreadsheets and plot out our life maps, or at least not with any degree of fulfillment. Because when we finally reach our destination, it may no longer even exist to greet us, and if it does, we may discover that we have no desire to be there.

The old Destinational Living approach also leaves no room for authenticity or individuation. A big reason why Jane was so unfulfilled working at her nonprofit was that it didn't have a whole lot to do with *her* and who she actually was. By her description, it never did. When we live Directionally, we make our lives personal.

The iterative nature of Directional Living is what allows us to stay in constant contact with our most current and authentic selves and to be responsive to our own changing needs and wants as well as those of the world around us. "Is this Directionally right?"—that is, Directionally right, *for me, right now*—is an inherently personal question. It's what infuses the unfolding of your life with authenticity and individuality, what makes it distinctly *your* life.

Right around this point in my explanation is when many UFOAs start to get very concerned that Directional Living means abandoning all ambitions. One woman in that workshop said she didn't aspire to be "a bump on a log." But I'm in fact saying quite the opposite. Ambition is great! I'm very pro-ambition here . . . so long as it is *yours*. We can conceive of ambition as simply a desire to make an impact; it means placing a high value on making a contribution to the world. In its Directional form, it's an internal call to more alignment, to more of yourself, to more life. Ambition is one of the greatest strengths of UFOAs, and it can be liberating. Unfortunately, though, it all too often gets distorted, and we become trapped by it. *Where* the ambition comes from and *why* we're ambitious matter. Did you inherit or absorb that aspiration, or did you generate it yourself?

We're keeping the ambition and changing the why and the wherefrom, which means going from *blind* ambition—fixed, generic, Destinational ambition—to *aligned* ambition—flexible, personal, Directional ambition, a concept we'll cover in more depth later on.

Forget Your Purpose

Another one of the workshop attendees was someone whom Claire Wasserman had known in her college days at Boston University and who was working as a bartender. Her name was Alexandria Ocasio-Cortez—"Alex," she told us—and she also identified as an Underfulfilled Overachiever. She'd been attracted to the workshop because she desperately wanted to "get unstuck." She didn't know what she wanted to do with her life and had no idea how to even begin to figure it out. She'd studied economics and international relations in college and had worked for the National Institutes of Health in youth leadership development, as well as other educational initiatives. But she'd started bartending because, as it turned out, she could make a more comfortable living that way. She was making good money and glad to be helping support her family, but she still felt a persistent emptiness. What Alex longed to do, she told us, was to build something lasting, something that mattered.

Most of you probably already know who AOC is. Maybe you've even read the numerous articles about her journey from bartender to youngest congresswoman in the history of the US House of Representatives. However, I'm sharing her story here—and from my perspective—because it is one of the best public examples of Directional Living that I have ever encountered.

I wanted to continue to support the women who had shown up for that first workshop and to see them through their transitions, so I offered everyone a steeply discounted rate for my private one-on-one sessions. Alex was among the first who followed up for additional coaching. She told me that she knew she had much more to give. But like so many other UFOAs before and since, she was perplexed over why she just couldn't seem to figure out her "life purpose."

I was not surprised to hear this. The idea of finding your "passion" or "purpose" has long been all the rage—regularly heralded as The Answer to career (and just general) malaise. I'd believed it, too. *If I could only find my passion . . . I'd finally be fulfilled*, I'd thought. But I have news: finding "passion" is not The Answer. I join a growing chorus of voices that have begun to challenge this notion and insist that passion isn't the magic pill it's been made out to be. At best, it's not that helpful, and at worst, it's actively debilitating. There's something far better on which to focus: your curiosity.

The first thing I told Alex? "Forget your purpose; follow your curiosity." Write it on the back of your hand, make it your phone background, frame it, or recite it every day—whatever you must do to remember this motto. If there's only one thing you take away, let it be this: curiosity > purpose.

Your curiosity is the best proxy for your purpose, for your Something Bigger. This is such an important concept in UFOA recovery that I've even given it a fancy name: the Purpose Proxy Principle. Your "purpose" isn't some static, immutable destination that you need to predetermine before you can begin living. You live into your purpose by following your curiosity. Your curiosity is your Directionally right.

Think of curiosity like hunger. As hunger is meant to tell you when you need nourishment, curiosity is meant to tell you when you need fulfillment. As craving a specific food is meant to show you where the nourishment is (like craving a steak when you need more protein or citrus fruits when you're deficient in vitamin C), being struck by a specific curiosity (like enrolling in a coaching training program or teaching a Get Unstuck workshop, as in my case) is meant to show you where the fulfillment is and where the Something Bigger can be found.

Only UFOAs, trained by years of Destinational Living, tend to think of curiosity as a frivolous distraction from their commitment to a linear, predetermined, up-and-to-the-right path. Your curiosity isn't there to distract you or to confuse you or to throw you off course. It's a hint. We want to cultivate our curiosity, not shun it or "overcome" it.

Alex's first assignment was to engage with and explore her curiosity. Here's what she and I did *not* do: we did not discuss strategic linear career paths, logical next steps, or ten-year plans. Instead, we started talking about what felt Directionally right for her individually and what her curiosity had been telling her. We focused on "just the headlights."

I asked her about the last time she'd felt excited, interested, engaged, eager to learn more, or just pulled by her curiosity. For her, that was easy. She'd worked as a volunteer organizer for Bernie Sanders in the South Bronx. She had loved the community organizing and activism, the grassroots stuff. She'd been thinking a lot about social change and was feeling invigorated (and frustrated) by it. She was enlivened by the political conversations and debates she had at the bar where she worked. She remembered, too, how inspired she'd been working for the late senator Ted Kennedy on immigration reform. In sum, it was politics and public service.

We talked about her other curiosities, too: education and literacy (she'd served as an educational director at the National Institutes of Health), entrepreneurship (she'd founded a company to develop representative urban literature for kids), international economic development (she'd studied abroad in West Africa). All of these were possible directions to explore. Even remaining in hospitality to see how that might evolve was on the table.

Staying open to all possibilities might sound overwhelming, but it doesn't have to be. I reminded Alex that our job wasn't to determine where she was going, only to determine what was the most Directionally right course of action at that moment. We didn't need to know where it would lead or where she'd "end up." And, in hindsight, it's very clear that in Alex's case, we couldn't have known!

I'd love to tell you that I'm so prescient, I looked at Alex and said, "Launch a political career by running for Congress against ten-term establishment candidate Joe Crowley." But the truth, and the key takeaway, is that there's no way she and I could have come up with the particular confluence of events that led to her becoming a congresswoman. At the time of our early sessions, the 2016 election and Trump's victory, which drastically changed the political landscape, hadn't even happened yet. If she'd insisted on a guaranteed destination, if she'd been powered by blind ambition and Destinational thinking as she navigated her path, *she would not be in Congress right now.* She would have missed the opportunity. *We* would have missed the opportunity to have AOC as a political leader and member of Congress.

Directional Living is like the scientific method but for life. You begin with a hypothesis—your best guess as to the direction of a loose Something Bigger. You design experiments, conduct tests, and collect data through your lived experiences, refining your life hypothesis as you go. If you have a life hypothesis that involves living on the beach, you may test that hypothesis by designing an experiment of sorts, such as renting a house on the beach for one month and collecting data on how aligned and Directionally right, or not, that is for you. The goal is not necessarily to permanently relocate to the beach but to find out whether you actually want to live on the beach, or at least whether you want to continue exploring that path. Once again, the goal is aligned truth and open-minded exploration, not blind adherence to the original hypothesis.

Success is in finding what's true, not in proving your original theory correct.

Alex and I looked at her various directions, her various life hypotheses, and the one that emerged as most Directionally right, the one where the curiosity craving was the strongest, the one she felt she couldn't *not* explore, was public service. I could hear the alignment in her voice. Sometimes one might need to explore several hypotheses in parallel, and sometimes they'll converge, but in this case, Alex's Something Bigger hypothesis—though not where it would lead— was clear.

Now it was time to "test" the public service hypothesis by taking the single next aligned action and iterating from there. The focus was on curiosity-led aligned actions in the direction of public service and, as in the scientific method, letting go of controlling the results. There were many low-stakes possibilities: attend some local community meetings, research what other former Bernie staffers were doing now, volunteer to support a grassroots activist organization that felt compelling to her. Forget your purpose; follow your curiosity.

And so she did. She found herself drawn to the Standing Rock protests that began in 2016. Instead of watching from afar, she and a friend borrowed a car and followed her curiosity to Flint, Michigan, and then to the Standing Rock Sioux Reservation on the border between North and South Dakota. It wasn't necessarily an obvious choice, and it didn't make a whole lot of logical sense to her at the time. This course of action didn't fit neatly into some larger strategic career plan. In fact, it didn't seem to have any clear connection to her "career" at all. Not only that, but it also meant taking days off work, which meant lost income, all for some completely undefined and uncertain outcome. If it feels Directionally right, I suggested, that's all you need to know. "It just felt like something I needed to do," she shared later.

Yep, Alex took a literal road trip based on a concept first introduced with a road trip analogy.

On the way to Michigan, she tried another spontaneous experiment—livestreaming their trip. Not for any specific purpose but because she was curious. What would it feel like to take all those conversations she was having privately and bring more people into the dialogue by sharing them on social media? Afterward, she would reflect, asking herself, *What felt compelling about this? How can I do more of this?*

As a result of her filming and sharing, she got a sense of what it was like to authentically communicate social issues that were important to her to "a public"—something at which, it turns out, she's incredibly gifted. She and her friend also used their videos to raise money on GoFundMe for supplies for Standing Rock protesters; they exceeded their fundraising goals—something at which, it again turns out, she's a natural. Today, her office runs almost entirely on small, recurring donations, and unlike for almost every other congressperson, the sum of these donations is enough that she doesn't have to do any cold-call fundraising at all.

On the very day she got home from Standing Rock, she received a call from Brand New Congress, an organization founded by former Sanders presidential campaign staffers. They were recruiting progressive and nontraditional candidates to run for national office without corporate or lobbyist money. And they wanted to know whether she would consider running for Congress. Following her curiosity to Standing Rock "opened a door I didn't even know existed," Alex wrote me. This is what makes Directional Living so powerful: when we let go of our Destinational scripts, living Directionally opens doors we didn't even know existed. How does someone make a huge decision like whether to run for Congress? Not in one fell swoop. With each conversation, at every step of the way, that person just keeps asking, "Is this *still* Directionally right for me?"

For Alex, a congressional campaign wasn't the most logical or strategic career move. It actually looked pretty insane. There were certainly no assurances about winning. In fact, a loss was all but guaranteed. And yet it felt Directionally right. Alex trusted that this was enough. The destination—the win—was irrelevant to the decision to run. The point was that she was a young, working-class Latina woman running for Congress. The direction was the point. It felt to her like she was exactly where she was supposed to be, doing exactly what she was supposed to be doing, even if she couldn't define exactly what that was. Regardless of what happened on election day, what new doors might this open? And then, against all odds, she did win. Alex became the youngest woman ever elected to Congress. It wasn't winning the election that made her feel unstuck, however. That happened way before the election, way before she became the AOC we know now, the national figure, the woman on the cover of magazines. It happened when she aligned with her Something Bigger, when she started making choices that felt Directionally right and found the flow of her aligned ambition. "It is pretty amazing to think about how far gone I felt then compared to where things are now," she marveled a year and a half before the election and eight or so months after we first met. "Sometimes things really are darkest before the dawn."

She hadn't "arrived" somewhere when she shared that—in fact, she was still bartending. And yet she felt that she had made it out of the "dark" and into a new "dawn" of her life. She felt clear and on purpose and *fulfilled*, even in the early days of her campaigning for an election that she thought she'd probably lose. Alex's story reinforces for us that "success" and fulfillment have little to do with achievement and everything to do with aligned direction.

As I was writing this chapter, Alex did an "Ask Me Anything" on Instagram and answered a question from a twenty-three-year-old seeking career advice. "Things started to unlock when I stopped trying to have a plan and started following my curiosity, even if it didn't make any sense in a 'career sense.' . . . Getting some title by some age is not the goal. . . . Building a good life . . . is much more important." A solid testimonial for Directional Living!

To this day, Alex continues to demonstrate Directional Living in one of the most Destinational of spaces. She's constantly asked about her plan, her political goals, where she's going, what's next—in other words, her destination. Senate? Cabinet? Presidency? Her answer is always some version of "I don't know," and I believe she's telling the truth. Even when she decided to run for a second congressional term, it wasn't a foregone conclusion. She told CNN's Dana Bash in 2021, "I know it drives everybody nuts. But the way that I really feel about this, and the way that I really approach my politics and my political career, is that I do not . . . set my course positionally." Positionally, in this instance, is another way of saying Destinationally; it's not about the title or the office or the "winning."

It's not that she thinks she will stay where she is, necessarily, or that she doesn't want to evolve and grow. It's not that she doesn't have ambition in the sense of a desire to have more impact. She most certainly does. It's just that it's not the calculated, hierarchical, blind ambition we're used to. It's aligned ambition, which requires in-the-moment responsiveness to the present reality. Aligned ambition is inherently circumstantial.

"I don't want to aspire to a quote-unquote higher position just for the sake of that title or just for the sake of having a different or higher position. I truly make an assessment to see if I can be more effective. . . . For me that's always what the question comes down to," AOC told *Vanity Fair* in 2020. In other words, she's asking herself at every juncture, *What is Directionally right? What's the most aligned next step for me?* And a big part of alignment is impact and contribution. Folded into the seeking of alignment are the questions

Where can I be of the most service? and *What am I the most uniquely well suited to do at this moment?*

Representative Ayanna Pressley, AOC's colleague and friend, has said that "she certainly did not set out to be an icon or even a history-maker. [But] I think it was her destiny." It seems so obvious in hindsight, and so hard to imagine Alex not knowing that this was her Directionally right, but I can testify that she truly did not know. This kind of Something Bigger exists for all of us—yes, you included.

The loudest fear I hear expressed by UFOAs about Directional Living is that if they set aside their focus on finding their purpose and follow their curiosity, they'll amount to nothing. We tend to believe that purpose and impact aren't possible without disciplined, diligent planning. But what AOC shows us is that Directional Living can, and often does, lead to more "success"—even the traditional kind of success that looks "impressive" to others. It doesn't at all have to mean giving up on making a significant impact, earning a meaningful salary, or even acquiring fancy titles. AOC proves to us that, with a different tack, our career paths can look good on paper *and* feel good inside.

People often ask me whether *I* saw what was coming for Alex. I had no idea what would unfold for her, but I did know that I was very excited about whatever it was. And I was confident, as I am with every client, that Directional Living would get her there—wherever "there" turned out to be. I knew that she had an incredible energy and spirit and brain—and that we would all benefit from her finding her most fulfilled, most aligned Something Bigger. I knew that I felt incredibly honored to support her in this process that isn't magic but can really feel like it. And I could tell she was ready. It's hard to define or quantify what readiness and willingness look like, but you know them when you see them. And you know if you have them.

What I think about more is that you don't run against powerful and moneyed interests for an office you're unlikely to win if you're focused on the end goal, on success and achievement. If you're all about the destination, you're not going to take the risk. You're not going to give up a week to go to Standing Rock and Flint, Michigan, "just because"—especially not when you're in the middle of focusing on "figuring out your next steps." You'd instead think, *I can't do that; that's a distraction.* You don't take the many controversial and powerful stances that AOC has taken in office if you're all about re-election and ladder climbing to the highest office possible. You don't let yourself be changed by experiences and adaptable to what the moment asks of you if you're prioritizing more achievements, more quickly. You don't respond to the specific circumstances of an unexpected (at least to many) 2016 presidential election result with Standing Rock and Brand New Congress if you're committed to a predetermined ten-year plan. And what a loss that would have been! No matter what your political views may be, AOC is an important voice and leader at a pivotal moment in the United States' democracy. What's more, she's expanded the country's view of who can, and should, run for Congress, and we're already witnessing the legacy of that.

Yet of all the significant and historical contributions that AOC has made, one of the subtlest yet most profound is the impact she's had on an entire generation of Underfulfilled Overachievers, who've seen themselves reflected in her struggle to build an authentic and fulfilling life and career. She's inspired UFOAs to believe that fulfillment and purpose are possible for them, too, and she's illuminated how the way to go about it might not be the way that we've always been taught. One of the reasons why I believe her story is so compelling to UFOAs is not because it is a rags-to-riches story, but, rather, because it is a misery-to-meaning story. It's not her success, or even her fame, that has moved us—it's her inspirited journey to finding her Something Bigger.

Getting Started

In *Big Magic*, Elizabeth Gilbert writes, "I've never seen any life transformation that didn't begin with the person in question finally getting tired of their own bullshit." I have found this to be unequivocally true, with one modification: it's not just tired of your own BS; it's tired of all the conditioned, inherited Destinational BS *and* the internal justifications and contortions that we go through in order to uphold it.

Ask yourself: *Am I tired of the Destinational BS? Am I tired of this F-ache?*

The biggest determining factor of a successful shift is willingness. That was so apparent with AOC. Or perhaps more accurately, it's a willingness to be willing, to imagine that it is in fact possible for you to live a fuller, richer, more fulfilled, more authentic, more meaningful, more impactful life that isn't such a struggle and so exhausting and anxious and F-acheful (a.k.a. a life that you actually love living and that actually feels distinctly *yours*). And if you're not there fully, that's okay. Simply wondering *What if?* is profound: *What if I don't have to try so hard to "figure it out" and "keep it all together"? What if a fulfilling Something Bigger exists for me? What if there is another way? What if it doesn't have to be like this?* Picking up this book alone is a powerful what-if.

If you still feel like it's all working for you, if the F-ache isn't big enough and painful enough, then read on, by all means—take a tourist approach. But get honest with yourself about the unlikelihood that anything is going to change. (And that's okay—there's no rush or requirement!) I would, however, like to offer you this saying from twelve-step groups: "We can always refund your misery." That is to say, you're welcome to go back to what you've been doing, to your Underfulfilled Overachiever Destinational approach, at any time. So you might as well give this a shot.

I'd like to offer a few final tips on how to approach the rest of this book before we begin your Directional Living process.

Most UFOAs take something like this book, something with exercises and assignments, oh-so seriously. And it is serious, but *feeling* rigid and serious won't help you cultivate curiosity. This can be serious *and* playful! It's for this reason that I give you permission to ditch the desk and professional attire here—the comfier you are, the better. We want to reach a different part of your brain for this, the one beyond the thinking mind, which is where UFOA habits live. That's a lot harder to access when you're doing all the "good student" things you're trained to do. If you have a choice, read on wherever you feel the most relaxed and spacious.

What we're about to do is a different type of learning. There are two learning principles—what I call the Principle of Exposure and the Principle of the First Draft—both of which I encourage you to utilize here. They'll help you process information not only more effectively but also with more ease and enjoyment.

The first principle, the Principle of Exposure, focuses on "exposing" yourself to the content and information instead of prioritizing "completion." The idea is to let the information titrate into your brain. The still-Destinationally-oriented UFOA brain likes to get stuck in "perfect," in "getting it right," and in "being finished," but the information osmosis that occurs through exposure is way more powerful and "productive" than you think. In other words, as you move through these next chapters, trust that you are taking in exactly what your particular brain needs to take in at this particular time. If something doesn't resonate, don't freak out. You're not doing it wrong. Maybe it will capture you at another time, or maybe it never will. Keep going. There's an expression: "Take what works and leave the rest." I encourage you to apply that nugget of advice throughout.

The second principle, the Principle of the First Draft, is about treating this entire process as if it is your first draft; you will have plenty of time and space for edits and revisions later. The classic analogy here is peeling back the layers of an onion. You are about to peel back the outermost layer, and a lot will be revealed. Then, maybe two months or even two years from now, you will peel back the next layer. You aren't going to peel the entire onion in this go-around. Don't even try. Take notes in pencil if that helps to remind you that your work here is a "draft." You're just trying things on right now, seeing what fits, and what feels good.

This isn't a race. (We all know how UFOAs love to turn everything into a competition!) Completing this book as quickly as possible so that you can move on to the next personal-development book would be quite the Destinational approach. You're not going to find your way to Directional Living by thinking Destinationally. Let the way you experience the rest of this book be the way you want to experience the rest of your life. The paradigm shift starts now.

72

Phase I: Recognize

Identifying the Problem

I once worked with two clients around the same time who happened to have uncannily similar stories. Aliya and Bea were in their mid-twenties and were extremely accomplished and ambitious. Each had attended a top university on full scholarship, taken on a double major and a minor, and graduated summa cum laude. Both had done so at the expedited pace of three years instead of the usual four. They were now a few years into their careers, one working at a major space exploration company, the other as an investment banker. They appeared to be thriving—on paper, at least—and would be considered ridiculously "successful" by most any outside observer. Yet both ended up in my office to report that they were in the depths of a "quarter-life crisis." Each was, in her own way, dissatisfied with her career, disillusioned with adulthood, confused as to how and when this had happened, and, like I'd been, ashamed that she hadn't been able to figure it out on her own.

Despite their similar backgrounds, though, it quickly became clear that they had come to me from completely different trajectories. One of them had been programmed to live Destinationally from a very early age, as I had. The other, however, had actually come into her Underfulfilled Overachieverness much, much later. After a few sessions with each, I learned that their experiences of their "successful" college careers had been vastly different. Aliya had been thoroughly fulfilled, energized, and engaged as an undergraduate, whereas Bea had been desperately unhappy, anxious, and lost. Both had racked up achievements, but they were not equally fulfilled by said achievements.

The difference was that, in college, Bea had been a UFOA living Destinationally, while Aliya had actually spent her undergraduate years living *Directionally*. How did I know? And how can you also learn to tell the difference between Destinational and Directional Living in your own life? Well, there's a test for that.

Bea

During our initial consultation, Bea explained her approach to her college career. She'd started as an econ major. "Honestly, my parents told me I should," Bea told me. "But it wasn't just them. I thought it sounded good or smart or something and would look good on a résumé and just be practical. Plus, econ was really challenging for me, and I figured the harder it was, the more impressive and worthwhile it would be.

"The second major," she said, "happened in my second year, when I met someone who was double-majoring in econ and engineering. That seemed even more impressive, and I realized that there were people doing even more than I was. I was worried that I wasn't doing enough and wouldn't stand out in a stack of résumés. It seemed like more majors would mean a better career. And then I read somewhere that environmental engineering was one of the highest-paid majors, so I declared that major as well. I thought it might get me a more stable career with better benefits and job security. I wanted to feel less anxious and more confident."

"Did it work?" I asked.

"Not even a little bit," she lamented. "After two years, I realized that I still didn't know what I wanted to do after college, and I started to get really scared about being able to get a job. At a career-guidance talk, I heard that employers were looking for people who have good 'soft' skills, so I added a minor in psychology to demonstrate I was a 'triple threat.' And I decided to graduate in three years instead of four. It felt like maybe then I'd get ahead."

"I'm curious—what do you think was your underlying motivation for all of these decisions?"

"I guess I kept just thinking that if I added more things to my résumé and could do them faster than other people, I'd be successful on the job market. I thought at some point I'd feel like I was okay and could relax. But I still don't feel successful or fulfilled. I just feel exhausted and empty."

The hallmarks of inevitably unfulfilling Destinational Living were stamped all over Bea's thinking and decisions. She was clearly an Underfulfilled Overachiever—restless, disillusioned, exhausted, and empty, with achievements up the wazoo. She was focused on the outcome of each decision and what it would "get" her at the finish line (the destination) with no regard for the getting-there part (the process). Bea was all about the résumé and only the résumé. When she described her college experience, she didn't talk about the classes themselves, the actual years of study and learning, or the knowledge and experience that she acquired. Her majors had nothing to do with what she, personally, cared about, what she was interested in, or what she was good at. She was consumed by what was most "impressive" and "practical," by how her choices would look to potential employers and compare with those of her peers. None of the choices she made were really *hers*. The great irony is that she thought, as most UFOAs do, that she was being risk-averse, "playing it safe," and being responsible and practical in her career choices. In fact, Bea did the riskiest thing she could possibly do: she essentially crowdsourced her career and her life. She bet her life on a game of Destinational roulette.

Aliya

Aliya, on the other hand, recounted her college experience to me with such joy. She talked about the all-nighters and how hard she'd worked and how stressful it had been at times. She wondered whether this was where she went wrong. But what I noticed most of all was how much the subjects she had studied lit her up when she described them to me. She fondly reminisced about the close and enriching relationships that she had developed with her professors. She laughed as she confessed that she didn't know what she'd been thinking in taking on so much coursework, but she also shared that every single one of her classes changed her and left an indelible mark. She remembered syllabi and reading lists and could recount specific assignments and what they'd meant to her.

When I asked Aliya how she had chosen aerospace engineering and gender studies, with a minor in creative writing, she simply stated, "I couldn't *not* do any of them." She'd been obsessed with all things space for as long as she could remember and found gender studies fascinating, especially given the male-dominated world of aerospace in which she was already immersed. She enjoyed creative writing and found it to be a helpful way to process her experiences. Meeting the requirements for the minor was a happy, "sort of fun accident," she explained.

"And all of this in just three years?" I inquired.

"Yeah, that . . . LOL. I'm such a nerd! I felt genuinely sad imagining having to leave school in May, so I decided to stay during the summers to keep taking classes and working alongside this professor who took me under her wing."

Blind Ambition vs. Aligned Ambition

Can you feel the difference in their approaches? What a contrast! Aliya and Bea are extreme cases, certainly, and I present them not because they're typical but precisely because it's often easiest to see these forces at play in the extreme. You need not have three college majors, or even have gone to college, to relate. Bea was like most of us: an Underfulfilled Overachiever living Destinationally. Aliya, by contrast, was decidedly not. Her decisions were suffused with joy and eagerness and excitement. The combination of aerospace engineering, gender studies, and creative writing was so obviously uniquely well suited to her. She chose to study these subjects because of what they sparked in her, and she intuitively trusted that whatever the direction those sparks took her would be enriching and rewarding, as well as meet her practical needs, financial and otherwise. There was not a single mention of anyone else's opinions shaping her choices. Aliya's college studies were as bespoke as Bea's were generic. This is what it looks like to be in alignment.

Aliya in college is an excellent example of Directional Living. She didn't enter college asking, as Bea had, "What degree am I going to graduate with, and how do I reverse engineer that process to achieve it as expeditiously as possible?" The destination—what each major would "get" her in the end—was simply not a factor for Aliya. The whole point for her was her actual attendance of the classes (direction), not what having taken the classes would represent (destination). She'd wondered, *What classes will offer me the most invigorating and inspired semester?* And she used *that* answer, as it continued to evolve from one semester to the next, to inform the navigation of her life choices and illuminate her direction, without becoming locked in the chokehold of needing to define the destination. Aliya picking up the course catalog and circling all the classes that interested her is the collegiate version of Doctorow's "only the headlights." She didn't religiously adhere to a master academic plan or a preplotted future career path. She just tended to her headlights.

Now, while Aliya had managed to stay out of the Destinational fray in college, she unfortunately quickly internalized it upon entering the professional world as a postgrad, which is why she ultimately came to me for coaching. Our work together consisted of reestablishing her Directional Living instead of finding it for the first time.

Still, what Bea's and Aliya's college examples illustrate is that ambition, drive, "success," and even intense work habits are not the problem. These two women were equally driven, with equally impressive results. By these measures, they are practically identical. Yet one was aligned and fulfilled, while the other was miserable. We can see, then, that it is absolutely possible to be ambitious, driven, accomplished, *and* deeply fulfilled. So what's the distinction? The difference is in the *why* (who's driving) and the *how* (approach) behind the ambition.

Consider the following questions.

1. Source: Am I outsourcing to others or insourcing from myself?

   Where is my motivation coming from?

   Who is doing the navigating?

   Is this personally aligned for me (versus broadly acceptable)?

2. Orientation: Am I focused on a destination/outcome or a direction/process?

   Where am I navigating to/toward?

   Is my goal a destination or a direction?

In the context of these questions, Aliya's college story is a model of *aligned* ambition—particular to her and no one else; she "insourced" her direction and path by following her curiosity and passions. Bea's college story is an example of *blind* ambition—numb to her own authentic alignment; she was driven by externally dictated outcomes.

My goal is to help you get clear on how to find and maintain a Directional, inner-guided orientation—it's the key to your fulfillment. Through our work together in the coming chapters, you'll learn to recognize when you're being driven, like Bea, by external, Destinational expectations. And then you'll learn how to practice Directional Living, as Aliya did in college, which is where all the good stuff—joy, peace, ease, purpose, meaning, and authenticity—lives.

The Four Omens

In these next few pages, we want to assess how you are specifically operating today so that we are clear on the contours of the problem in your particular life before we begin addressing it. Don't worry if you're not yet sure of your answers to the questions I just posed. With practice, you may be able to answer them quickly and directly, but remember that these are not questions we're used to asking ourselves. In fact, it's likely that, until a chapter or so ago, you didn't even know they existed! It's perfectly normal not to be immediately sure about how to articulate what these concepts mean to you and how they show up in your own life. As promised, I have a simple test to help.

Through years of studying Underfulfilled Overachieverness and tracking the signature patterns of Destinational Living, what I've found is that there are four key indicators of Destinational thinking that, when present in one's decision-making rationale, reliably predict unfulfillment. I call them the Four Omens. They are: Obligation, Objectivity, Optics, and Outcomes.

Omen #1: Obligation (the "shoulds")

KEY QUESTIONS: *What "should" I do here [according to others]? What would others advise?*

KEY INDICATORS: *"should," "should not," "supposed to"*

EXAMPLES:

"I should get a PhD."

"I should have ten thousand followers."

"I'm supposed to like yoga."

"I shouldn't eat carbs."

"I should be married."

"I should own a house."

"I should be further ahead in my career and life
than I am."

I'm certainly not the first person to talk about the "shoulds." Karen Horney wrote about "the tyranny of the shoulds" back in the 1960s. This is not a new idea, and yet here we are sixty years later, still tyrannized by the shoulds; clearly, we're not getting it. This is usually the lead omen, and one of the easiest to spot. Rarely, however, does it stand alone.

Omen #2: Objectivity ("objective" logic and strategy)

KEY QUESTION: *What's the objectively "right," smartest, and/or most strategic move?*

KEY INDICATORS: *"logical," "I think," "right," "smartest," "best," "most strategic," "the most sense"; superlatives*

EXAMPLES:

"The logical choice would be to stay at my 'very good' job."

"The smartest choice would be to accept his marriage proposal. He's the right kind of person to marry."

"It makes the most sense to maintain friendships with this group of people and not burn any bridges."

"It's objectively the right choice to buy instead of rent."

Omen #3: Optics

KEY QUESTIONS: *How will it look? How will it be perceived? What will it say about me?*

KEY INDICATORS: *"people will think . . . ," "it will look like I . . ."*

EXAMPLES:

"I can't quit my job without another job lined up; how will I explain the gap on my résumé?"

"If I break up with my boyfriend right now, I'll look like an asshole."

"I can't disagree with that approach. People will think I'm not a team player."

"I need to breastfeed. Otherwise, people will think I'm a bad mom."

Omen #4: Outcomes

KEY QUESTIONS: *What will this get me? How will this advance me?*

KEY INDICATORS: *if-then statements; future tense; "so that"*

EXAMPLES:

"It will look good on my résumé."

"I'm taking this job now, so that in five years, I will be able to do XYZ."

"If I accept this speaking opportunity, then I will be taken more seriously and get more publicity."

"I need to get engaged now, so that I can have children by thirty-two."

"If I pay my dues now, then I'll be able to have any job I want later on."

Let's return to Aliya and Bea, this time through the lens of the Four Omens to perform what I call the Fulfillment Test. To conduct a Fulfillment Test, you evaluate your decision-making rationale for the presence of Four Omens. If any of the Four Omens are present, it is a Fulfillment Test fail. If none of the Four Omens are present, it is a pass.

Bea's college-major decisions were, of course, an overwhelming Fulfillment Test fail. Here's a review of how each of the Four Os showed up in her decision-making:

> **Obligation:** She believed that she "should" have multiple majors, graduate faster, demonstrate "soft" skills, and choose marketable majors; her parents said she "should."

> **Objectivity:** She thought her majors were objectively "good" and "hard."

> **Optics:** Her motivating force was how her decisions would be perceived by others; she pursued what she thought would make her look like an "impressive," well-rounded "triple threat" on her résumé, and she was consumed by the desire to stand out, to do more, and do it faster than everyone else.

> **Outcomes:** She was focused on what her choices would get her and where they would lead—to a good career, more job security, guaranteed success, more confidence, and less anxiety.

Aliya, on the flip side, was a Fulfillment Test pass. None of the Four Omens informed her decision-making. There was no use of the word *should*, no discussion of the logical or objectively "right" path, no mention of optics or how something would appear to others, and no focus on outcomes or any specific destination.

Aliya and Bea both came to me with a career focus. But the

Fulfillment Test works equally well when applied beyond the professional realm. Even though the work we do is usually the part of our lives that we most closely associate with "ambition" and "overachieving," an Underfulfilled Overachiever doesn't stop being an Underfulfilled Overachiever just because they're not in the boardroom or a Zoom meeting. In any area of life, they can zero in on an identified and esteemed destination and become laser-focused on reaching it. You can take the UFOA out of the office, but a UFOA they'll still be.

One of my clients worked hard for over a year and beautifully learned how to navigate her career Directionally. She was thriving, with a rich and fulfilled professional life. I was proud of her and all the work we had done together. Then one day she arrived in my office for a session and wanted to discuss a new decision she was facing: motherhood.

"I think it's time to start trying to have a baby," she told me flatly. Her lack of enthusiasm was palpable.

"Um . . . you don't sound very excited about that," I responded.

She confessed that she felt like she "should" have a baby, that she might regret it if she didn't, that she might miss her opportunity and then it would be too late. She told me that it seemed like the next logical step in her relationship and also, practically speaking, like the appropriate time. She insisted it was time to "grow up" and "put down roots." She reported that "everyone" said their life gained purpose and meaning when they had a baby. And, finally, she thought that it would look like she was selfish and immature, like something was wrong with her, if she didn't have a baby soon. People would wonder.

Let's run her decision rationale through the Fulfillment Test by assessing the Four Os.

Obligation: "I should have a baby."

Objectivity: "It's the logical next step and the practical, appropriate time."

Optics: "I'll look selfish and immature and like something is wrong with me if I don't."

Outcomes: "This will give me purpose and meaning and prevent regret."

Externally driven and Destinational, this client's decision-making process was a Fulfillment Test fail—and potentially an extremely consequential fail at that. This was not an aligned, authentic, inner-directed, and Directionally right decision; she was "shoulding" herself.

When I pointed this out, she looked aghast. But later that night, she left me a voice note saying how relieved both she and her partner were. They felt like they had been given permission to wait. I believe her exact words were: "Thank fucking God! What a shit show that would have been! This is so liberating!"

Once again, the problem here has nothing to do with either the issue itself or what ultimately reveals itself to be the aligned right-for-her decision. At that moment in my client's life, the aligned decision was clear. But just two years later, the aligned decision changed: that same client told me she was pregnant and that this time the decision had passed the Fulfillment Test with flying colors.

Now that you know about them, you'll probably start seeing the Four Omens everywhere. And they aren't only for "big" or "serious" decisions. I encourage you to pay attention to the small unfulfill-ments, too.

While writing this book, I went out to dinner with a friend. As we perused the menu, she said, "I should get the salad. That's obviously the healthier choice."

My Four Os alarm bells were blaring: the obligatory "should" followed by the "objectivity" of the "healthier" choice. I knew she wouldn't be satisfied with her meal (and would end up eating mine!): "Okay," I said, "but what do you *want* to order?"

Without hesitation, she replied, "They're known for their homemade pasta, which sounds way better and more interesting."

I'm happy to report that she ordered the pasta. I then told her, "You know this is going in my book, right?!"

If you apply a Destinational Living strategy to one aspect of your life, you're likely to apply it to other, if not all, areas—work, romance, marriage and partnership, parenting, family, friendship, volunteer and community commitments, hobbies, home life, exercise, food, politics. It pervades everything!

Your Turn: Taking the Fulfillment Test

The best way to determine whether you're living Destinationally is to give yourself a Fulfillment Test by scanning for the Four Omens in a decision that you're currently deliberating, have recently made, or chose in the past. The limit of this test is, of course, that we are really only assessing one choice. But I've found that we can reliably consider the rationale of just one decision to be a microcosm for our default decision-making strategy. The way we make one decision is often the way we make all (or at least most) of our decisions. In short, tell me about a decision you've made, and I'll tell you about your life.

1. **Choose a decision to test:** Think of a decision that you've just made or are currently in the process of making. You can also think of a past decision that stands out to you, especially one that was fraught or difficult to make. Don't overthink this by trying to choose the most perfect decision to assess. (I see you, UFOAs!) Any major-ish life decision will do. You are welcome to repeat this test over and over (and, in fact, I expect you will), so whatever decision comes to mind first is fine. If you're drawing a blank, here are some ideas: a school selection or major, a job offer, a move, a marriage or committed partnership, a family-planning choice, a career change. It can be any decision, big or small, but for our purposes, in this context, it's best if it is substantial enough that you spent a fair amount of time thinking about it and can remember your thought process.

2. **Observe:** Write down your rationale for the decision. How are you thinking about, or how did you think about, that decision? What factors or elements are influencing or influenced your decision? Do your best to set aside the Four Omens for now. Pretend that you've never heard of them before. The goal here is to simply explain your thinking and what factors are or were influential.

3. **Analyze:** Reread your decision rationale and look for elements of the Four Os. You may want to go through it with a highlighter. Alternatively, if you do this digitally, you can also do a word search for the key words as a starting point.

Omen #1: Obligation ("shoulds")

_____

_____

_____

Omen #2: Objectivity + logic

_____

_____

_____

Omen #3: Optics

_____

Omen #4: Outcomes

4. **Results:** Did you observe any Os?

    a.   Yes = Fulfillment Test *fail*

If you see any of the Four Omens, then your decision is very likely to result in unfulfillment (or did result in unfulfillment) and would be considered a fail. The good news is that there's a whole book for this. Keep reading!

    b.   No = Fulfillment Test *pass*

Congratulations! It's likely that this decision will be a fulfilling one for you (or was a fulfilling one for you). This means that it is (or was) personally aligned for you and Directionally right.

    But also . . . are you sure?!?! If you suspect that you're an Underfulfilled Overachiever and the UFOA stories thus far have resonated with you, unless you've previously spent time doing work around making aligned and process-oriented decisions (or unless you're coming back to this after having already read the whole book!), then I have to tell you the hard truth that it's unlikely that you'd pass the Fulfillment Test, so check your work!

If you're getting stuck, try explaining your thought process to a partner, and have them keep an ear out for the Four Omens.

One way smart, strategic thinkers can get muddled here is by imagining a scenario in which the Four Omens are all present, which may not actually reflect the true experience of the decision-making process. It's important to remember that we are assessing your *actual* decision-making rationale, not your *hypothetical* rationale. This is why it's key to start by articulating your decision in your own words, without any concern for the Four Omens.

Take this very book, for example. One might think, *I should write a book.* One might think that doing so will "get" authority and respect. One might think that it's the next logical step in a successful career, that it's an objectively "important" thing to do. My own decision to write this book could have been an Underfulfilled Overachiever decision, as any decision can be. Can I think of ways that I could have "shoulded" myself into this book, that this could have been an "objectively right" instead of Directionally right decision, that optics could have driven my decision? And can I envision being totally and exclusively focused on what publishing a book would get me? Absolutely.

However, I can assure you that I put this project through a very thorough Fulfillment Test before I undertook it. (Also, how messed up would it be if I hadn't?) In fact, on my most challenging days, I went back to the Fulfillment Test to make sure that the project still passed and that my frustration was really just standard creative frustration, not inklings of misalignment. What was true for me throughout was that even if my most wonderful editor had called and said that I was off the hook for the book *and* didn't even need to pay back my advance, I *still* would have gotten up the next morning, and every morning thereafter, to work on the manuscript until it was done. I would have self-published (if that's what my headlights had shown me) or done whatever else it took to put this book out into the world. This was a thing that, as it came into being, I couldn't *not* do (and trust me, at times I wished this weren't the case). For me, this book was an aligned and Directionally right decision. What would have failed the Fulfillment Test was any attempt to convince myself that I should *not* write this book.

Just a few years earlier, however, writing this book had in fact failed the Fulfillment Test! After a literary agent reached out to me, we had a few meetings, worked up a book proposal, and talked timelines and titles and tone, but I was unhappy and uninspired. Almost immediately, and with great disappointment, I halted the whole project, with no idea whether there would ever come a time when it would truly pass the Fulfillment Test.

This is also why we can't assess Underfulfilled Overachieverness from the outside. No one except the person in the driver's seat can know what is aligned and Directionally right, because there are no universally correct choices. I cannot know whether a client's decision is a fulfilling or unfulfilling one without access to their inner dialogue and deeply listening to their decision-making process. And you couldn't see my book on a shelf and know, without hearing from me, whether writing it was a fulfilling or unfulfilling, Directional or Destinational endeavor for me. We sometimes assume that high-achieving people must be so satisfied with their lives or, conversely, so jaded and miserable. Neither is something you can know from the outside. This is why I highly discourage diagnosing anyone except yourself as a UFOA, unless you have intimate access to their inner life.

As in any good recovery process, though, thoroughly assessing *yourself* is a critical first step. Hopefully, you now have a clear picture of the problems with Destinational Living and the way this conditioning dictates your life. You are familiar with the symptoms of Underfulfilled Overachieverness and are armed with a diagnostic tool to evaluate yourself quickly and easily. Since you're here, you've in all likelihood realized that you are, indeed, an Underfulfilled Overachiever who is living Destinationally. Congratulations! You're ready to move on to the next phase and are one step closer to meaningful and lasting fulfillment. You now know that the quandary of what will and won't fulfill you is actually not as mysterious as you once thought.

Phase II: Align

Recovering Your Inner Sense of Direction

Here's some common life and career advice that you *won't* ever hear me say: Follow your bliss. Trust your gut. Do what you love. You can do anything you put your mind to!

It's not that any of this is bad or wrong, per se—it's just unhelpful. When I was lost and struggling and people said such things to me, I always felt like responding, "If I knew my freaking bliss or what my 'gut' was telling me, don't you think I'd be doing that already?!"

During my coaching training, I was surprised when I was instructed to ask a particularly frustrating question for UFOAs: "What do you *really* want?" That might seem a useful inquiry at first blush, but try asking an Underfulfilled Overachiever that question (say, you yourself, perhaps!) and you'll very likely get a blank and panicked stare.

Again, it's not that it's a bad question. We do want to unearth that answer! It can be a useful thought exercise. But what all these pieces of advice miss is that most UFOAs aren't harboring, at least not consciously, secret dream lives that we just need permission to build.

The challenge is that we have absolutely no goddamn idea what we want. And it's not because we're indecisive or incapable of listening to our "gut" or because we don't love anything at all; it's because we've forgotten *how* to know what we desire. (Remember my whole tissue box meltdown in CVS?) We have limited (if we're lucky) or no access to what our "gut" is telling us, because we've spent our whole lives exorcising that from our awareness.

Before we can talk about what it is that we really want—our aligned ambition—we must learn how to determine that in the first place—that is, how to get into alignment with ourselves. In order to do that, we have to start with an understanding of the human operating system—the mechanics behind the way the mind, body, and truest self all work together (or not).

Like a computer operating system, we have a master infrastructure running behind the scenes to keep us alive and well. We have the "survive" part, whose charge is safety and security. It says very helpful things like "Get out of the way of the speeding car!" It also says plenty of unhelpful things, such as "You might die if you leave this job! Never leave!" and "It's way too dangerous to run for political office; you're never going to win."

We also have a more existential "thrive" part that craves Something Bigger. This is the "follow your curiosity" part, and it says things like "Go see about this coaching thing" and "Go to Standing Rock."

Our survive part is primitive and ancient and operates from the amygdala, which is why it's sometimes called the "lizard brain." The thrive part is a more recent evolutionary development, and it operates from the more evolved prefrontal cortex of the brain. As a result, the older survive part gets precedence, while the thrive part—the part we're interested in when it comes to our big, beautiful lives of meaning and purpose—operates as more of an afterthought; it is much quieter and harder to hear. And it means that we're predisposed to viewing our lives and ourselves through a fearful lens. In psychology, this is known as negativity bias.

It also doesn't help that the lizard brain lacks nuance and can be pretty heavy-handed on the alarm system. It sees anything new or uncertain as a big fat threat. It doesn't understand that the "threat" of potentially feeling embarrassed while asking someone out on a date or interviewing for a job is not the same as the truly life-threatening experience of being chased by a large wild animal.

And so because the survive and thrive parts haven't figured out how to play nice together, they often feel at odds within us, which makes decision-making difficult and stalemates likely. The thrive part wants things like authenticity, originality, and creativity, which inherently require embarking on something new that we aren't entirely sure how to do. That freaks the hell out of the survive part. The survive part's motto is "Better safe than sorry," while the thrive part says something more like "No risk, no reward."

Think of the beginning of a romantic relationship. Your thrive part is screaming, "Yes! Intimacy and curiosity and resonance! Meaningful and rich connection! Stay! Explore!" Meanwhile, even if this person is your most perfectly compatible soulmate, your survive part is yelling, "No! Too much exposure and vulnerability and uncertainty. Way too much risk and potential for failure. I predict pain and suffering ahead! Major liability. Run!" Which part do you want to heed?

Despite being designed for protection, our survive part most often appears in our lives as a very loud, very intimidating fearmonger that holds us back from our Something Bigger, which is why I refer to it as the Fear Self.

All of that is the standard human operating system for most

people. However, there's a whole other level of additional confusion and dysfunction for UFOAs, which makes the thrive part that much more difficult to hear: a system bug called Destinational Living.

Destinational Living is inherently a fear-based survival philosophy. It's all about security and preservation and minimizing uncertainty by attempting to control outcomes, an approach that the Fear Self just loves to promote.

And yet we UFOAs have been convinced that Destinational Living is not a "survive" strategy but a "thrive" one. The crux of Destinational Living's success in holding so many of us hostage for so long is that it crosses our wires and has us listening to the Fear Self coo about Destinational Living as if it were our thrive part. It acts as if it is advocating for our fulfillment, for our authenticity, for our Something Bigger, when in fact it keeps us conforming, compliant, and stuck. Our operating system got hacked. It's become a million pop-ups promising big, thriving fulfillment, but in reality, it's just dead links and porn.

How to True Yourself

How, then, do you follow your thrive part without getting clobbered by your Fear Self?

You true yourself.

In carpentry, the word *true* is a verb. To "true" means to restore to accuracy or alignment. If something is warped, misshapen, or crooked—a floor, a table, a wheel, a house—you might true it, returning it to its original and intended state and bringing it back to life.

This is where we begin our recovery: by trueing our warped, Destinationally distorted thinking. To do that, we have to learn how to distinguish between our fear-based thoughts, which are the vast majority, and those that are inviting us to thrive. This trueing process is crucial. Proper calibration is the key to Directional Living. Inversely, without a functioning thrive part, fulfillment isn't possible.

A trued thrive part—or what I'll call the True(d) Self from here on out—is the most essential and basic tool of Directional Living. Some people call this intuition, a gut feeling, or inner knowing; please use any language that works for you. Call it Fred if you like. In fact, I will suggest that you name this part for yourself eventually, but for now, I'll refer to it as your True Self.

Your True Self powers your Inner Navigation System, which provides personalized, constantly updated directions that guide you and keep you on your most aligned, Directionally right path toward fulfillment. It is the part of you that holds the answer to the question "What do I *really* want?" It speaks to you through your curiosity and through the things that light you up and bring you joy. This is where we go to insource (instead of outsource) our decision-making. This is what leads us out of the trap of blind ambition and into our unique aligned ambition.

This True Self is extremely resilient. It makes adjustments in real time. You can reroute, make a bunch of U-turns, get lost, and still find your way to your Something Bigger. Even if you have never had a "gut response," don't believe in intuition, and have one hell of a loud Fear Self, I assure you that if you have a Fear Self, you have a True Self, too. And we can find it. It's not precious. It doesn't hold a grudge.

I can't overstate how thrilling this is. This is not an urban legend. This is what you've always wanted—an authority to tell you what to do with your life! You just didn't know you already freaking had it! There *is* a part of you that knows exactly what to do with your life! It knows where the fulfillment and the purpose and the meaning are, and it wants to give you step-by-step instructions to get there. Once it's trued to you, it's extremely trustworthy and dependable.

I know what this sounds like: "The answers are inside you!"

Nothing used to piss me off more than when someone said that to me. And I confess, that is what I'm saying. Yes, it's beyond annoying when platitudes have some merit. But bear with me. I promise I'm not sending you off on some aimless treasure hunt in the wilderness of your inner world. The book doesn't end here. The True Self is way more practical and less amorphous than it sounds, and I will teach you a specific step-by-step process for finding and utilizing it.

Allegra

I used to offer one-off single sessions—I called them A/B sessions—in which I'd focus on one timely fork-in-the-road, inflection-point decision with a client and evaluate the most aligned option-A-or-option-B choice. These sessions usually addressed things like where to go to grad school, which job offer to accept, stay-or-go relationship moments, and potential big moves across the country or abroad. But I also got requests for A/B sessions on topics such as baby names, wedding venues, business branding, and even book titles. And every January, without fail, I'd get a request for a session on medical residency specialty.

By way of explanation for those who don't know how the medical training system works in the US, you attend four years of medical school and then apply to residency programs in a specific specialty. You rank your program choices, and on a single day in March called Match Day, you and the rest of your peers find out where (and, stressfully, sometimes *whether*) you'll be going on to residency training. There is almost always a lot of strategy involved: which specialties are the most in demand versus which are under demand, which locations are currently considered more or less desirable, et cetera. As one can imagine, the residency program in which a candidate finally ends up has a tremendous influence on the trajectory of their career, including their workload, income, and quality of life.

Predictably, it was early in the new year when Allegra reached out to me. She was finishing her four years of medical school, and the question of residency loomed. She was intensely torn between neurosurgery and psychiatry. She described her confusion as kind of wanting to choose both and kind of wanting to choose neither. She'd always known that she was going to be a doctor, and not only a doctor but a brain surgeon. Her parents had met in medical school, and her mom was a heart surgeon. Allegra had been fascinated with biology, especially the biology of the brain, since she was a kid. She'd gotten every premed internship and neurology research lab position that she could. She characterized herself as "obsessed with neuro" and had never considered pursuing another specialty.

Until, that is, she herself needed a psychiatrist. Halfway through med school, she'd found herself burned out, depressed, and anxious. She'd been shocked to discover that she didn't like medical school—because she loved school! She loved biology! She'd been looking forward to this period of her life for as long as she could remember. Medical school, she'd assumed, was going to be her moment to shine. It wasn't. Still, she reasoned, it was necessary and worth it; she wanted to be a neurosurgeon, and this was the path to that dream. She knew she could "push through and make it happen," because that's what she'd always done. And so that's what she did—in part with the help and support of a psychiatrist. Through their work together, things became manageable.

But that's also when she got confused. Allegra really admired her psychiatrist—she was brilliant and intuitive, and her care had changed Allegra's life, so much so that the aspiring neurosurgeon found herself daydreaming about becoming a psychiatrist. This, in Allegra's mind, was a big problem: it was a distraction. She tried to ignore it. But when it came time to begin interviewing for residency programs, she decided that she "might as well" interview for a few psychiatry programs "just to rule it out." Except doing so only made her more conflicted.

Before our session, Allegra sent me several extensive spreadsheets with multiple tabs categorizing the pros and cons, the stats and probabilities, and the advice she had received from a wide swath of people. (This sort of documentation is quite common among UFOAs.) And when she walked into my office, she had bags under her eyes (also common). I thanked her for sharing the documents with me. Then I gently broke the news: it was unlikely that anything in them was going to give her any clarity. I asked for her permission to set them aside, literally and metaphorically, and to try something different. She reluctantly agreed.

If you ever had to do that exercise in grade-school science class where you put a magnet near a compass and use it to alter the needle's direction, making it spin around and around, then you know what an Underfulfilled Overachiever's Inner Navigation System is like when one shows up in my office. Allegra was spinning from a lifetime of unattended fear dominance and Destinational Living. The Buddhist author and teacher Ethan Nichtern wrote in his book *The Road Home* that "inhabiting a human nervous system is kind of like living in a house where the doorbell and the burglar alarm make exactly the same sound." Our primary job in UFOA recovery, and specifically what we will do in the trueing process, is to learn how to discern between our burglar alarm (Fear Self) and our doorbell (True Self).

Your Turn: The Trueing Process

There's a model of decision-making based on the classic children's game called warmer-colder. If you ever played this as a child, you may remember that one player hides an item and directs another player to find it by calling out "Warmer!" when they are headed in the right direction and getting closer to the hidden object or "Colder!" when they are headed in the wrong direction and moving farther away from the hidden object.

Here we are going to partake in a personal version of this widely known game. The Inner Navigation System works like a warmer-colder barometer that shouts "Warmer!" when you're Directionally right and "Colder!" when you're Directionally wrong.

TRUE SELF

Let's begin by thinking of something that you know you love completely and unequivocally—a person, a place, a thing, an experience. This should be something or someone or somewhere that makes you feel completely yourself, completely at ease. It makes you happy just thinking about it. It could be almost anything: a pet, a vacation destination, a place where you used to live, a job you loved, a mentor, a childhood caretaker, an activity, a song, a friend, one specific memory, or even an outfit that always makes you feel amazing.

Don't overthink this. Anything that pops into your head right now will do the trick. You can always refine or adjust later. Let it be iterative!

Thing I love:

_____

Allegra knew hers immediately: her grandparents' cabin in Maine, where she'd spent her summers growing up. I asked her to close her eyes and describe it. She told me about how mesmerized she was by the coast and the ocean, the texture of the wind, the quality of the sun, the taste of the ice cream and the fresh corn and the tomatoes, the smell of basil in the garden, swimming with her cousins, the outdoor shower, her grandfather grilling, playing cards with her grandmother.

Describe the thing you love and/or list key words you associate with it:

_____

_____

_____

I asked Allegra how it felt to think about this place and what sensations, what emotions, she associated with it.

Being free, peaceful, calm, completely myself, playful, relaxed, joyful, happy, safe, cared for, nourished, nurtured, carefree, grounded, satiated.

How it makes me feel, emotionally:

_____

_____

_____

I asked her to stay there and continue holding this place in her mind but also to scan her body and see what she noticed, specifically in comparison with how she felt when she arrived for our session. This, for many of us UFOAs, can be challenging, as we're not used to looking for information within our bodies. We tend to go straight to our thinking minds.

I offered what I noticed had seemed to shift in Allegra, saying, "Your breath slowed down, your shoulders dropped, your facial muscles relaxed, and your voice changed." Then, I asked if any of it felt true to her.

She nodded and added: *My brain is less busy, my stomach feels less knotted, and the straitjacket feeling has disappeared.*

How it makes me feel, physically:

_____

_____

_____

Remember these physical sensations. Take an inner snapshot. How would you summarize who you are here?

Allegra's response: *In Maine, at the cabin, I'm just completely me, at home in myself, and YAY!*

Who are you with this thing? (Choose one or two key words.)

_____

_____

_____

This sense of being at home in yourself, of assurance and peace, is the "Directionally right" guidance of your Inner Navigation System. Your doorbell is ringing! You can recognize your True Self and your most aligned way forward through these sensations. This is how your True Self says, "Come on, this way!"

This voice, this "completely me," this "yay" feeling—that for Allegra we'll call "Maine"—is your "warm." Your job is to heed this common piece of advice shared in recovery spaces: "Go where it's warm."

FEAR SELF

Let's compare that warmth with its opposite: the "colder" and "Directionally wrong" guidance of your Fear Self.

Think of another person, place, thing, or experience. Only this time, choose one you hate, one that feels icky and gross and uncomfortable. It doesn't have to be extreme or traumatic; in fact, I wouldn't recommend that—take care of yourself here. But it does need to be something you unequivocally dislike.

Keep it simple. Maybe a job you hated. Or a food you don't like. A sound that makes you cringe. A politician who makes your blood boil. Your most dreaded chore. Or maybe a time in your life that you know you just don't want to go back to.

Thing I hate:

_____

Allegra came up with "Dr. Dick," a notoriously arrogant and condescending attending physician she'd had to work with on one of her rotations. His reputation had earned him this nickname, which was, conveniently, also his real name. I watched her hands furl into fists at the thought of him.

Describe the thing you hate and/or list key
words you associate with it:

_____

_____

_____

Now, the same questions as before.
When you think of this thing, how do you feel?
Allegra's answers: *Ick. Cringe. Angry. Trapped. Small. Uncomfortable. Just NO.*

How it makes me feel, emotionally:

_____

_____

And then, underneath that, what are the specific sensations in
your body? Scan your body, starting at your head.
Allegra slowly scanned her body: *Hot. Head throbbing. Shoulders and neck tense. Breath shallow and fast. Stomach hurts. Nauseous.*

How it makes me feel, physically:

_____

_____

Almost done. Again, remember this feeling, as uncomfortable as
it is. Take that inner snapshot.
How would you summarize who you are with Dr. Dick?
Ick was Allegra's summary.

Who are you with this thing? (Chose one or two key words.)

_____

_____

These uncomfortable and dissenting feelings are how your "colder" and "Directionally wrong" instructions show up in your body. This is how your INS warns, "Wrong way! Turn around!"

BRINGING IT TOGETHER

Let's bring your personal navigational poles together. Fill in your key words below, as Allegra did.

Directionally Right/ Aligned/Warmer	Directionally Wrong/ Misaligned/Colder
Maine	_Dr. Dick_

Now, pick up each of these items, one at a time, and try them on in your mind as you might try on an item of clothing. Toggle back and forth between the two. For Allegra this looked like: _Maine, Dr. Dick, Maine, Dr. Dick._

As you do, pay attention to how this _feels_—emotionally but also sensorially. The physical sensations are the shortcut to a trued INS calibration.

Maine, Dr. Dick, Maine, Dr. Dick.

Directionally right, Directionally wrong, Directionally right, Directionally wrong.

Warmer, colder, warmer, colder.

Can you tell the difference between these two poles? What do you notice?

For me, when I need to recalibrate my INS, I might toggle back and forth between the obvious-but-failproof-for-me *coaching* (warmer) and *Google* (colder). This reminds me instantly what both my Directionally right and my Directionally wrong feel like.

My quick-reference code for True Self physical sensations is "light and right" (warm) versus "hard and heavy" (cold).

For Allegra, what resonated with her were two key words taken from her previous summaries: yay versus ick.

What might your two key words be?

_____ vs. _____

Below are Allegra and my personal warmer-colder summary charts, or legends, as examples, followed by your own warmer-colder legend to be completed based on your work in this chapter.

Allegra's Legend

	Directionally Right/ Aligned/Warmer	Directionally Wrong/ Misaligned/Colder
Reference	Maine	Dr. Dick
Feeling	yay	ick

Megan's Legend

	Directionally Right/ Aligned/Warmer	Directionally Wrong/ Misaligned/Colder
Reference	coaching	Google
Feeling	light and right	hard and heavy

Your Legend

	Directionally Right/ Aligned/Warmer	Directionally Wrong/ Misaligned/Colder
Reference		
Feeling		

The first law of Directional Living—and therefore of UFOA recovery and aligned ambition—is to choose the path of most ease, not the path of most struggle. We go *toward* "light and right" and *away* from "hard and heavy."

I love how the late artist and writer Anne Truitt put it: "The hallmark of a decision in line with one's character is ease and contentment, and an ample, even provision of natural energy." If a decision brings you ease and contentment and naturally energizes you, then you can be confident that it is an aligned decision for you.

This is an important shift because it's the inverse of what Destinational thinking tells us. It may also require some getting used to and some reprogramming on our part. Many of us feel "ease" and immediately register "wrong." That's how I operated for a long time.

When I finally followed my curiosity to my first coaching training, I loved it so much and felt so damn good there. It was the epitome of ease, contentment, and natural energy. But this feeling was so foreign to me that it somehow felt wrong. It felt like I was cheating. *This can't be right,* I thought. *Meaningful and worthwhile things don't feel like this—they feel hard and challenging.* No pain, no gain, and all that. It took me four months to go back for the second coaching training in the series, though I thought about it every day.

Another client adored advanced math theory. It came naturally to her, and she could get delightfully lost in it for hours. Yet, in college, she chose prelaw, as it required more effort and discipline to keep herself engaged and focused—in other words, it was much "harder" for her. She believed that the more challenging choice must surely be the more valuable one.

Can you think of a time when you did something that felt hard and heavy and that you didn't really want to do, especially if you chose it over something you really *did* want to do?

We're conditioned to think that suffering is virtuous and that the more suffering there is en route to the destination, the larger the pot of fulfillment and success upon arrival. A core belief of UFOAs is that it has to be difficult to be worthwhile.

In Directional Living, we reject this outright. Suffering is not a prerequisite for meaning. There's no gold star or fulfillment bonus for extra struggle. Toiling and suffering don't make your accomplishments any more impressive.

Please know that putting an end to equating suffering with value is not the same as avoiding challenges and difficulty. Certainly, sometimes the "hard" things are not only necessary but aligned. In a bit, we'll get to the difference and how to discern aligned, Directionally right "hard" from misaligned, Directionally wrong (unnecessary) "hard."

For now, think about what this means for your life. The light-and-right path is the path of your most meaningful and unique impact. The hard-and-heavy one takes you *away* from that. If you could embrace this wholeheartedly, what might that be like? What would change?

PUTTING YOUR INS INTO PRACTICE

Now it's time to put our Inner Navigation Systems into practice.

Let's get back to the question at hand: Option A or B? For Allegra, that was a choice between neurosurgery and psychiatry.

I asked Allegra to try on option A (neurosurgery) in her mind. I told her to close her eyes and imagine that it was Match Day and that she was opening the envelope containing her possible future as a neurosurgery resident. I encouraged her to think about going through her day as a neurosurgeon.

The next step, just as we did in the original calibration, is to drop down from your head and into your body. This is not a thinking brain exercise, so right now we're not interested in what your brain is telling you. It will definitely start chatting (or shouting) if it hasn't already. Tell it we'll come back to it. If you need to jot down what it's saying to reassure your brain that you won't forget, go ahead and do that. Then return your full attention to the information in your body.

What does your body feel like emotionally and physically? Is it closer to "Maine" or closer to "Dr. Dick"? "Yay" or "ick"? Is it warmer or colder?

Allegra told me that imagining her life in neurosurgery made her feel hot and nauseous, as if she might cry. Her shoulders slumped, and she looked like she was caving in on herself. She admitted that she felt trapped and stuck. She told me she hated that this was the answer, but she was decidedly not in "Maine."

Don't jump to conclusions about what this answer might mean or what you think you "have to do" now as a result. This is simply information, not a commandment from on high. We aren't analyzing yet!

Option A: _____

    Emotionally: _____

    Physically: _____

    Closer to warmer or colder: _____

Now, I told Allegra, *let's switch to option B, psychiatry. Same approach: Try it on in your mind. Envision opening the envelope holding a psychiatry residency match. Imagine your day as a psychiatrist—what you're doing and how it feels to be doing it.*

Drop down into your body. Again, this is not a thinking exercise.

What does it feel like emotionally and physically?

I watched Allegra's face soften and a small smile appear. Just sitting there with her eyes closed, she already looked so much brighter.

She told me that she felt inspired and free and much more relaxed. The nausea, the hotness, and the tears were all gone. She felt peaceful. "Shit," she said. "It's Maine."

Option B: _____

    Emotionally: _____

    Physically: _____

    Closer to warmer or colder: _____

Allegra realized that her most aligned, Directionally right path was psychiatry. Said another way, psychiatry is what she *wanted* to do.

Maybe you've also reached a similarly significant insight about your own life. If so, record it.

My warmer, more aligned, Directionally right path is:

_____

What I want is:

_____

Or maybe you're still feeling confused. That's okay, too. In fact, it's perfectly understandable and not uncommon. Just like you wouldn't start with a three-hundred-pound deadlift on your first visit to the gym, there's no need to go from not even knowing you have a True Self to making a major life decision like quitting your job in a matter of pages. The point here is to give you the tools to build your True Self muscle by doing the equivalent of some five-pound reps. Practice making small decisions on a daily basis. Let's start right now. The process is the same, whether we're talking about moving to another country or buying a box of tissues.

MAKING ALIGNED DECISIONS

Starting Small

Begin by coming up with a list of five smallish choices you can make using your Inner Navigation System. Keep it very simple. You might write down decisions such as what TV show to watch tonight, what to eat for dinner, what exercise class to sign up for, where you'll go on your next vacation, what outfit to wear tomorrow, or whether to click "Buy" on whatever item is still sitting in your online shopping cart.

Example:　　　*Bike to work*　　　*or*　　　*walk to work*

1.

2.

3.

4.

5.

Instead of trying to "figure it out" using your brain, practice making each of these decisions by tuning in to your INS, as we did in the last section with Allegra. Refer back to your own answers for help. Can you find that light and right, yay feeling?

It's not enough to just know what decision is the aligned one; you must also actively *choose* that choice. You'd think this goes without saying, but the UFOA Fear Self can be very wily. (We'll get to more strategies for dealing with that soon.)

Come back to your list and circle the True Self decision once you've actually enacted it. If you can't find your warmer choice—as I struggled to with the Kleenex boxes in the CVS aisle—don't do what I did and have a meltdown. Move on to the next decision in your day and try again.

Each of these choices alone is low-stakes, but cumulatively, the impact becomes significant. The more you use your internal sense of direction to make small, daily decisions, the more natural and automatic it becomes. Eventually, it'll be your default.

This practice also has a secondary purpose. With each aligned decision you make, you're giving your INS another true coordinate, making it stronger and more accurate. This is what will allow it to grow loud enough and clear enough for those future three-hundred-pound decisions.

Spend the next few days using your INS to make as many small decisions as possible. Because we UFOAs tend to be motivated by getting "credit" for things, keep a list of all the decisions that you're making using this method so that you can see your progress. This will also motivate you to seek out additional opportunities to practice making aligned choices. Aim for five a day.

Consider these questions as you go: What do you notice about this process? When is it easier and more intuitive? When are you resisting or having trouble accessing your internal sense of direction?

The Pushback

From my perspective, Allegra and I had arrived at a place of exceptionally clear True Self guidance: she was going to be happiest and most fulfilled by choosing the psychiatry route. Allegra admitted that psychiatry resonated in her body. She agreed that her INS was telling her this was her right choice. Or, more accurately, she agreed that this was the result of the exercise we had done together. But that didn't mean she was ready to check the psychiatry box. She wasn't at all convinced that the solution to her dilemma could be so simple.

This is extremely common. The Inner Navigation System is as simple and straightforward as it gets: Go where it's warm. Go toward what lights you up, what makes you feel alive, and what makes you feel like yourself. Go away from what drags you down. And yet, because of this, a session rarely ends there. For UFOAs, this is one of those simple-but-not-that-easy situations. Knowing your Directionally right decision isn't always enough, at least not this early in UFOA recovery, because you have become so used to rejecting your True Self guidance.

The work is not just to identify your True Self answer but to actually enact that True Self decision. Your most aligned action does you no good if you don't then take that action. So why isn't it easy? Why can't we end the session here? We have an "answer," don't we?

Part of it is that it takes time to trust the voice of your True Self. It does get easier, especially as you start to see positive results. You have years of "the harder, the better" programming to undo. But the bigger impediment is your built-in saboteur: the Fear Self.

Allegra understood that what she really wanted was to study psychiatry. As she sat in my office, however, all of her "logical" reasons for why psychiatry was still the "wrong" choice flooded back into the forefront of her mind. Suddenly, she was rattling off a long list of other "very important considerations" we hadn't factored in.

She told me that neurosurgery was still the smarter choice. "You just don't choose psych over neuro," she said. Neurosurgery was more competitive and more impressive. If she did psychiatry, she insisted, people would think she just couldn't hack it in neurosurgery. People would respect her less. And she'd make so much less money. She really should have a higher income after all these years of study. You didn't win awards for cutting-edge psychiatry. You became a renowned neurosurgeon, not a renowned psychiatrist. She ended with "Yes, I should definitely do neuro."

"Good," I told Allegra. "We want to confront all of these. And you absolutely can choose neurosurgery. I have no vested interest in either choice. But hear me out. I strongly suspect this is your Fear Self throwing a temper tantrum." I explained how her Fear Self would get increasingly desperate and say and do anything to keep her "safe" (read: stuck) in Destinational Living compliance. It wanted to breed confusion, crossing her True Self and Fear Self wires. The bigger and truer her inner guidance was, the louder the Fear Self would become. "It sounds like your Fear Self is throwing a fit, and it's a good indication that we've identified an aligned and True path for you," I said. "Otherwise, your Fear Self wouldn't have anything worth resisting right now. Remember, your Fear Self is not interested in your fulfillment, nor is it invested in your Something Bigger."

Allegra looked unconvinced. I told her not to take my word for it, because there was another way to reliably distinguish between the Fear Self and the True Self.

I assured her that we would address, one by one, each of the points she had made. But first, I asked her to notice how she had just offered a lot of justification and robust analytical reasoning—that's the Fear Self. The True Self doesn't justify or offer lengthy explanations; it simply *is*. Directionally right alignment is "just because"; it's never defensive. The True Self's attitude is best summed as "I don't need to explain myself to you."

The anxious, survival-focused Fear Self lives in the analytical, thinking mind, and so it communicates verbally. We tend to hear it more readily because Destinationalism has taught us that linear, verbal understanding is the basis of good decision-making. In fact, the opposite is true.

The True Self resides in the body. It is the part entrusted with our thrive instinct, as we just experienced when we Trued ourselves, and as Allegra experienced when she let herself access her "Maine." It's a sense of warmth and alignment and light and right. We're taught that "sensing" is less reliable and less trustworthy, but it's actually *more* so. In order to thrive, we must drop out of the fearful "survive" mind and into the warmer-colder sensations of the Inner Navigation System, which lives in our bodies.

There's a saying that's attributed to various spiritual teachers, including both Robin Sharma and Ram Dass. As that adage goes, "The mind is a wonderful servant and a horrible master." Instead of the thinking mind as "master," we want to appoint the True Self in that role. The mind is best thought of as the executive functioning needed to serve the True Self's Directionally right path. In other words, your mind is an unreliable narrator and not a trustworthy leader or decision-maker. Your analytical mind doesn't dependably outsmart your Fear Self, despite what we're often told. Because when you let your mind drive, you open up the possibility—or the probability, really—of fear doing the steering.

That doesn't mean your big brain is useless and should be put out to pasture. Far from it. We just want to assign it appropriately. My thinking mind is articulating the ideas in this book and organizing these pages, but it's not a reliable decision-maker when it comes to *whether* it's aligned and Directionally right to write the book in the first place. I want to enlist my mind to serve my True Self's decision-making, not lead the decision-making itself. Once Directionally right is determined, we can put the mind to work.

So the first thing we want to notice is how the decision-making voice sounds: Is there a robust verbal justification involved? If, as in Allegra's case, there's a lot of mental processing and explaining going on, then it's very likely that you're voicing your Fear Self. The second step of this Fear Self assessment is to consider what it feels like, by bringing in your calibrated INS to help evaluate these statements. In the same way we can try on a choice (such as neurosurgery versus psychiatry) to assess warmer-colder alignment, we can also try on thoughts and beliefs to determine where they fall on our inner truth barometer.

For Allegra, we began with trying on the statement "I want to be a neurosurgeon."

Your statement to interrogate:

_____

Hold that thought in your mind, as we did with Allegra's Maine cabin and lecherous professor. Drop into your body for the emotional and physical sensations. We're not interested in any verbal and analytical arguments that spring up. This is not a brain exercise. We're still sensing.

Think about where this falls on your warmer-colder navigation spectrum. Does it feel more like "yay" or "ick"? Light and right or hard and heavy?

For Allegra, it was all "ick" and very cold.

Is your statement warmer or colder?

_____

When we put the thought *I want to be a neurosurgeon* through her personal True Self detector, it registered as decidedly "not aligned."

Allegra and I went through the same process with several of her other statements, including "People would respect me less," "I won't win awards," and "You don't choose psych over neuro." All got the same result: "Ick."

Next, I suggested that she try on the thought *I'm choosing psychiatry* and repeat it to herself until she got a read in her body. Once again, I could see a tiny smile forming. "That's warmer," she said. "There's a lot of 'yay.'"

So now we've run through a couple criteria to identify the Fear Self:

• How it sounds: Is there a robust verbal justification?

• How it feels: Is this thought warmer or colder?

There's also a third line of defense against an insidious Fear Self, and perhaps, reader, you've already guessed what it is. Did you notice that Allegra's pro-neurosurgery argument was littered with the Four Omens of the Fear Self and the harbingers of Destinational Living? As we continue to focus on our alignment, we can use the same Four Os to distinguish between the Fear Self and the True Self, between the burglar alarm and the doorbell. Remember, the Four Omens are Obligation, Objectivity, Optics, and Outcomes. The first three are indicators of outsourcing our decision-making (instead of insourcing it from our True Self), and the last one, Outcomes, is evidence of Destinational orientation.

Let's break down the Four Os in the case Allegra made for neurosurgery. She'd said:

I should choose neuro. It is the smarter choice. You just don't choose psych over neuro. Neuro is more competitive and more impressive. If I do psychiatry, people will think I just can't hack it in neuro. People will respect me less. And I'd make so much less money. I really should have a higher income after all these years of study. You don't win awards for cutting-edge psychiatry. You become a renowned neurosurgeon, not a renowned psychiatrist. Yes, I should definitely do neuro.

Omen #1: Obligation (the "shoulds")

KEY QUESTIONS: *What "should" I do here [according to others]? What would others advise?*

KEY INDICATORS: *"should," "should not," "supposed to"*

ALLEGRA'S OBLIGATION OMEN:

"I should do neuro."

"I should have a higher income."

The obligatory "shoulds" are generic, programmed, external-to-you navigational commands. They are usually the easiest Fear Self indicators to spot, once you know what to look for. Of course, when it's your own "should," it doesn't always feel obvious. In your own brain, it sounds reasonable and reassuring. It's persuasive. But think about who uses the word *should*—bullies! The Fear Self is the ultimate bully with all its self-directed "shoulding."

The takedown for the "shoulds" is: "Says who?"

To this, Allegra responded, "Everyone!" And then: "My parents. My classmates? Maybe my professors?"

"That's not going to cut it!" I told her. "The only acceptable answer here is 'My True Self' or 'My Inner Navigation System,' and you can only give that answer *if* it feels like Maine, like warmth, like yay. In which case, it's a *want*, not a should."

Omen #2: Objectivity ("objective" logic and strategy)

KEY QUESTION: *What's the objectively "right," smartest, and/or most strategic decision?*

KEY INDICATORS: *"logical," "I think," "right," "smartest," "best," "most strategic," "the most sense"; superlatives*

ALLEGRA'S OBJECTIVITY OMEN:

"It is the smarter choice."

"You just don't choose psych over neuro."

Again, the pushback to this: "Says who?" and "According to whom?"

To which, this time, Allegra responded, "I have no idea."

Or I could have asked: "Smarter, better, and most strategic for whom?" and "According to what criteria?"

Because nothing I'd seen or heard from Allegra suggested that neurosurgery was the smarter choice for her if what she was seeking was fulfillment, purpose, and meaning.

There is no single smartest, most logical, most strategic, or universally right decision in personal life choices. Anytime we're leaning on "logic" or some nebulous universally right choice, we're out of our True Self, and we're outsourcing.

Omen #3: Optics

> KEY QUESTIONS: *How will it look? How will it be perceived? What will it say about me?*
>
> KEY INDICATORS: *"people will think . . . ," "it will look like I . . ."*
>
> ALLEGRA'S OPTICS OMEN:
>
> "People will think I just can't hack it in neuro."
>
> "People will respect me less."
>
> "Neuro is more . . . impressive."

The use of optics and perception is a core tactic of the Fear Self because it preys on our evolutionary need for belonging to ensure our physical safety and security. What if you get kicked out of the community and are more vulnerable as a result? But, in this context, the choice of what medical specialty to practice is unlikely to meaningfully threaten your ability to remain in polite society.

How something may or may not be interpreted by others has absolutely no bearing on whether a decision is aligned for you. Factoring in optics as part of your decision-making process is a sneaky way of relying on external, faceless "people" to navigate your life on your behalf. That's old UFOA-compliant behavior that leads to unfulfillment.

If you want to challenge your thinking on this, you can start by getting specific about "people." *Who, exactly, will think this?*

If you can actually think of someone who is important to you saying something like this (e.g., "My best friend, Bob, told me he'd definitely think less of me"), which is rarely the case, then you can have a conversation with that person to explain your real criteria and inner dialogue to them.

About the rest of these faceless "people," you can ask:

- *Do I know with certainty that this is what "they" will think?* (Hint: No.)

- *Is there another possible way that people could interpret this choice?* (Hint: Yes, like the real one!)

For Allegra, it's just as possible that "people" will think, *Wow! Her passion must have shifted to psychiatry. It's so amazing that she gave herself permission to follow her curiosity for such a big and meaningful and personal decision, instead of staying fixated on outdated beliefs she had about herself. That's so impressive.*

This is also to say nothing of the fact that "people" are usually thinking about us a lot less than we tend to think they are. And whatever they may or may not believe about our decisions tells us more about *their* own Fear Self than about the quality of *our* choices.

Our actual goal here, though, isn't to deliberate the merit of each statement—what people will or won't think—but rather to simply identify each one as a Fear thought. That alone is enough to rule it out of our decision-making criteria.

Omen #4: Outcomes

KEY QUESTIONS: *What will this get me? How will this advance me?*

KEY INDICATORS: *if-then statements; future tense; "so that"*

ALLEGRA'S OUTCOMES OMEN:

more money

more awards

more renown

Lastly, outcome orientation is a dead giveaway for Fear Self sabotage. If we're making decisions Destinationally, we're in Fear Self mode.

Here, Allegra's Fear Self is talking about the outcomes she'll miss out on by choosing psychiatry: less money, no awards, no renown. If she chooses neurosurgery, her Fear Self argument goes, then at *that* destination there will be more money, more awards, more renown.

Even if that ends up being accurate, it still neglects the fact that making a misaligned choice may mean years of misery before Allegra sees any of that money or those awards, and then still more misery after that. And it's also a fallacy that choosing neurosurgery *guarantees* money, awards, and renown!

Again, even if that Fear Self's Destinational prediction is true today, we have no idea what will happen in the next ten, twenty, thirty years. Maybe neurosurgery is taken over by robots and ceases to exist as a specialty. Meanwhile, AI fails to crack the nut of psychiatry, and incomes for psychiatrists skyrocket. Or maybe Allegra chooses psychiatry and goes on to develop a new diagnostic methodology that changes the landscape of mental health forever. And she wins a Nobel. I'm not saying that any of these are likely, nor does it need to be this extreme. Maybe Earth continues to be such a stressful place to live that the demand for psychiatrists increases exponentially alongside her income. The point is that the Fear Self claims to offer Destinational certainty, but the reality is that it's making promises it can't always keep.

To challenge:

- *Can I know with certainty that this outcome will happen?* (Hint: No! Certain outcomes are extremely rare, no matter how likely.)

- *What's one other way this could turn out?*

- *What happens in the meantime? What will the process be like?*

You'll notice that I'm not addressing the accuracy of each of Allegra's statements, such as which specialty garners more respect or makes more money. I don't personally have any of the associations that Allegra has with psychiatry or neurosurgery. I'm not addressing the content of each comment, because it's irrelevant. That's a game of whack-a-mole. The Fear Self will always come up with another justification, and we'll get so exhausted and be so busy combating justifications that we'll never make a choice at all, which, to the Fear Self, is a win. Our job here is not to get lost in the arguments themselves but to recognize the nature of the temper tantrum so that we can exclude it from our aligned decision-making. Be content-agnostic.

And please don't take this as a sign that I agreed with Allegra's interpretation or took what she said about these specialties as fact.

This was her subjective interpretation at that point in her life, and it was far from her own True Self interpretation.

The Traps

For Allegra, this screening for the Four Omens indicated a clear Fulfillment Test fail and confirmed, for the third time, that her preference for the neurosurgery choice was stemming from her Fear Self, as:

1. There was a robust verbal justification coming from her thinking brain;

2. It felt colder to her Inner Navigation System; and

3. All of the Four Os were present.

I put it to Allegra like this: "Does it make sense to you that if you choose neurosurgery right now, using the logic you just outlined, your motivation for that decision would be based on Destinational thinking and other people's ideas about your choice? And that any decision made from this place is very unlikely to lead to fulfillment and very likely to lead to the F-ache? Do you see how you'd be choosing a fear-based, externally directed suggestion over your own internal, Directionally right, True Self guidance?"

Allegra nodded, and we sat in silence for a few minutes, letting this information settle. Choosing what other people "know" over what you know—what other people want over what you want—is a form of self-abandonment.

There are two other confusing, seemingly contradictory traps that the Fear Self sets up for us, and we want to look out for them as well. It was at this moment in our session that Allegra, astutely, identified the first one. Now we're getting to the advanced Fear Self and True Self discernment lessons.

"Here's what I don't get," she told me. "I know I'm scared to choose neuro because it's really hard. What if I really can't do it? What if I fail? I know that I feel less of that with psychiatry because it seems like it will be harder to fail and will have less pressure, less competition. Coming into this conversation, I thought that my fear of failure with neuro meant I should lean in to that, not lean out of it. After all, isn't the point not to let fear dictate my decision? How do I know that psych is *actually* a True Self choice and not just the 'safer,' cop-out, avoidant option based on my fear of failure?"

Such an important distinction: Was it—neurosurgery, in this case—"good" hard and scary in an aligned way? Or was it "bad" hard and scary in a misaligned way? Was this a True Self "just NO" (like Dr. Dick), an authentic red flag signaling that something was genuinely out of alignment? Or was it a Fear Self no that was keeping Allegra stuck and sabotaging her (like the one that had kept me stalled on the coaching training)?

Our Fear Self loves to complicate things and disguise itself as our True Self, and this is one of its favorite ways to do so. The remedy is to return to the three Fear Self–related identifying tactics that we've practiced already. Let's work the psychiatry option this time: Was psychiatry a true yes or a Fear-based and avoidant yes?

1. How it sounds: *Does this yes come from my brain or from my inner sense of direction? Is it a verbal justification, or is it a felt sense?*

Allegra didn't have many words for why she wanted to do psychiatry. Of course, we could conjure up some logic here, but we don't want to reach for it. We just need to decipher whether the yes inherently comes with a lot of justification, which would be the Fear Self talking.

Allegra had yet to offer me any diatribes about why psychiatry was the smarter thing to do, only a clean, even, uncomplicated, no-justification-needed yes, repeatedly.

That's our first affirmation it's a True Self thought, a true yes, not a Fear Self–manipulated one.

2. How it feels: *What does my Inner Navigation System say?*

You know this process by now! Tap in to your INS and try on the True Self yes—psychiatry, for Allegra. Feel into how that option shows up inside your body. Is it warmer or colder? For Allegra, it was warmer.

If Allegra had drummed up a big justification for psychiatry, she would have now needed to do the third test, the Fulfillment Test, to scan for the Four Omens, as she had done with neurosurgery. But since that wasn't the case, this step was skippable.

The key is that we know it's the True Self when there is an *absence* of the Fear Self.

Where Is the Freedom?

If you've done all of the above and it's still unclear whether the mind-set at hand—"I should do neuro," in Allegra's case—is a wolf in sheep's clothing or the Fear Self masquerading as the True Self (or if you just want to be extra, extra certain), there is a pair of magical confusion-busting questions we can ask that cuts through all the Fear Self shenanigans: *Where is the freedom?* and *Where is the relief?* What is the scenario that gives you the greatest sense of freedom and/or relief? Is it in doing the thing or in not doing the thing?

One way to experiment with this question is to imagine that the decision has already been made for you. Do you feel freedom? Do you feel relieved? Or do you feel disappointment and regret? We're always going for freedom in Directional Living. Freedom is a prerequisite for fulfillment.

I asked Allegra, "What if I told you that you couldn't do psychiatry? That it had somehow already gotten filled up and was no longer an option? How would you feel?"

As you might expect at this point, she looked panic-stricken.

On the flip side, I asked Allegra how she'd feel if I told her that neurosurgery was filled and she had no choice but to do psychiatry. "Yeah, I feel relieved," she acknowledged. "I don't have to disappoint anyone, *and* I get to do psych."

In Allegra's scenario, her perceived "safer" choice was also her true yes. Neurosurgery would be "bad" hard, as in forced, misaligned, Destinational, and definitely-not-fulfilling hard.

That said, it is absolutely possible for a True Self yes to also be the perceived "harder" thing. The truest, most aligned path for you is sometimes the (perceived) harder one. This was not the case for Allegra, but if another UFOA had come to me with the exact same scenario and beliefs, we may have discovered that choosing neurosurgery was the most aligned True Self move. It's not whether there will be challenges; it's determining which part of you is advocating for the "harder" choice and whether that's the part you want leading the way. It's about the *why* of the hard. Is it "Four Os" hard—in other words, hard because it's an obligatory "should" based on optics and outcomes and "objective" rightness? Or is it hard because it feels vulnerable and uncertain?

One former client reached out to me for a "sanity check." She'd been offered a new position in her organization and was debating whether to take it. She was an engineer and a product manager working at a large social media company, and the new role was to lead the misinformation team. It was 2019 and about a year out from the 2020 US presidential election. Rampant misinformation on social media had become a critical, high-stakes issue. This would be a very difficult job. The need to fill this role was dire; the team was in disarray. The last manager had quit. Half the engineers had defected. Burnout and dissatisfaction were high. There was no vision or strategy or product road map, not to mention that, in terms of real-world consequences, this was probably as close to a life-and-death issue as one was going to find working at a social media company.

Simply put, no one wanted this role. Her mentor had told her that the team's mandate was an impossible one and that she would not be set up for success. It would be a huge mistake, and she'd be committing career suicide, he said. It wasn't even revenue-generating, he reminded her; if anything, it would be revenue-reducing. A team like that would never be prioritized or elevated or well-resourced.

All of this was true, she knew. Who needed that kind of stress and frustration? Plus, this would be a lateral move—no promotion, no raise. She was already managing a thriving team that she adored. She was the happiest she'd ever been at work. For the first time in her career, she'd achieved something like the illusive "work-life balance." Why would she disrupt that?

And yet, in idle moments, in the shower and at stoplights, she'd found herself thinking about the other team and the role—the impact she could have, the engineers she'd recruit, how she'd reorg the team, what she'd tackle first, how she'd frame the problem, the business case she'd make for the team's impact, and how she'd get buy-in from the company's most senior leaders on the importance of this work. It had occurred to her that she may never again have the opportunity to work on something so important, so historically significant, and even democracy-saving.

As she recounted this last part to me, she shook her head aggressively, as if trying to Etch A Sketch away her thoughts about what the new position could mean. "I want to want to say no and not make my life unnecessarily difficult, but something isn't letting me," she lamented.

So what was going on here? Was the true, aligned, and Directionally right path staying where she was content and considered successful? Or was it signing on for possibly the hardest but likely the most important professional challenge she might ever face?

We got down to work. For starters, we knew that the only big verbal case being made in her brain was why she "should" *not* (notice the first of the Four Omens) take the new role. Once again, this was a pretty good indicator that the Fear Self was on Team Stay, and this was therefore a plus-one for the aligned path being the new role. To further assess her Inner Navigation System's responses, I suggested that she try on both scenarios—not just in her mind's eye but by actually going through the motions of having made each decision. I encouraged her to see whether it felt warmer or colder to indulge all those ideas she'd been having in the nooks and crannies of her day about the potential of the new role and team. I told her to spend a few days acting as if she'd accepted the new position and was already in the process of relaunching that team. She might write out her vision, her task list, her priorities, the people she'd recruit, and even the meetings she'd want to schedule. Make some spreadsheets, start a new tab on her project management tool . . . go nuts! She bemoaned a bit the logic of doing extra work for a job she didn't have and probably wouldn't accept but agreed to try it.

A few days later, she reported that her brain felt like it was exploding with ideas. She said she remembered why she wanted to be in tech and entrepreneurial environments in the first place. She felt more connected to her *why* than she had in years. She was working on a problem that *mattered*. When she gave herself permission to do the thing she thought she should *not* want to do—the thing that seemed like the hardest, most stressful undertaking—somehow, much to her surprise, she felt light and right.

Next, I suggested that she spend at least twenty-four hours acting as if the opportunity had been rescinded. I wanted her to spend some time feeling into the contrast between the two scenarios. Just twelve hours later, I got an email from her that said, "This sucks. It feels awful. Definition of hard and heavy. So. Much. Colder. Every time I remember that the decision has been (hypothetically) made for me, I feel panicky and sick."

She knew the true, aligned decision: accept the challenge of rebuilding the new team. It was the Directionally right kind of hard.

For a final confirmation, I asked her the magic confusion-busting questions: *Where is the freedom?* and *Where is the relief?* For her, she felt so relieved when she let herself want the more uncertain and way more challenging thing that also really mattered to her. She felt so much freedom in tackling this issue head-on instead of cringing from the sidelines. It would be worth it, whether the team failed or succeeded, whether the decision advanced her career or not.

In the end, it was clear that the truest, most Directionally right thing for her, not to mention for the organization and the product, was to accept the position as the new director of misinformation tools. This was not the answer she had anticipated or wanted at the start, but it was definitely the most aligned one for her in that moment.

We don't want "hard" for the sake of hard or, for that matter, easy for the sake of just *not* hard. Aligned "hard" usually comes from vulnerability and from pushing yourself out of your comfort zone, as it did for my engineer client. Misaligned "hard" usually comes from self-abandonment and from "shoulding" ourselves, as it initially did for Allegra. It's a different texture of "hard." Can you feel the difference?

This is why discernment between the Fear Self and the True Self is tricky and why we go through the Fear Self assessment process. We must locate the place that is free from the Fear Self's machinations. Each case is unique unto itself, and the aligned decision in any given case will be different for each person.

Near the end of my session with Allegra, I asked her whether she was feeling confident in her choice of psychiatry. I saw her eyes well up, and she deflected with the "I'm not crying, you're crying" meme.

"I'm confused about something else," she said. "This absolutely does not feel like 'ease.' This feels really fucking hard. I've spent my whole life identifying as a future neurosurgeon. And now I'm just . . . not?! That can't be right. What about light and right and all that?"

This is the second seeming contradiction. "Path of most ease" isn't the same as "easy." Decisions can be hard and still be Directionally right for you. Even if a choice is aligned for you, you may still have a lot of uncomfortable and complicated feelings around it. Many decisions come with a sense of loss alongside possibility, but that doesn't mean they are misaligned choices. There was intense grief in letting go of my sense of myself as a "Googler," despite the fact that this identity nearly killed me. Leaving was terribly difficult *and* absolutely aligned for me. Grief often comes with even the best, most exciting life changes and decisions: graduating, moving, marrying, parenting.

I asked Allegra to also consider whether the feelings and emotions that were coming up for her felt *opposed to* the "yay" feelings of psychiatry or simply existed side by side and in tandem with them. In a True Self choice, the uneasiness and sadness don't cancel out or replace the light-and-right feelings. They exist simultaneously and in parallel. They are simply another piece of the aligned, Directionally right decision. They belong there; they're not in conflict.

This is because those feelings are *also* coming from your True Self. Grief is not a defensive, protective, Fear Self feeling. It's a vulnerable, openhearted one. It's the *refusal* to grieve and to process change—change is a kind of loss—that's a Fear Self response. It's a breakup. Allegra needed to mourn and to let go of the future she had imagined with neurosurgery. If you're asking yourself, *But who would I be without this thing?* that's a pretty good indicator that your most aligned path is to find out who you are without that thing.

Directionally right choices can still require some challenging conversations and actions, and that can make the aligned path feel not so easy. Allegra was going to have to tell a few professors and mentors that she was no longer pursuing neurosurgery. They were likely going to be surprised, perhaps even disappointed. Whatever your aligned path, it's often the case that there will be additional work and study involved in any transition, which can be daunting. It can sometimes feel like you're starting over from the bottom. But you're not. All the prior knowledge that you thought was in service to something else can still help you—in fact, it's already helped you get to a place where you were able to uncover the next aligned iteration of your life.

The thing to remember is that these feelings do not necessarily mean you're doing something Directionally wrong. Having an uncomfortable feeling is not a reason to reroute something you've intentionally and thoughtfully determined is a trued choice for you. And we need to be vigilant here because the Fear Self loves to capitalize on these less desirable feelings and say, "See! I told you! Bad choice! As you were! Homeostasis!" UFOAs often first need to say no to something, and potentially let someone down, in order to say yes to their Directionally right. But since such a potentially disappointment-inducing conversation is hard, Underfulfilled Overachievers may take their discomfort as a sign that this is not the path of most ease and therefore not a Directionally right choice after all. Uncomfortable, uneasy feelings are like the weather. The ease we're talking about with trued alignment is deeper and sturdier and outlasts those uneasy, passing weather fronts.

We can always come back to our magic confusion-busting questions if we're getting disoriented: *Where is the freedom?* and *Where is the relief?* If there is freedom and relief on the other side of the challenging conversation or action, then it is still your most aligned and Directionally right path.

Was there freedom and relief on the other side of letting go of neurosurgery for Allegra? Her answer was yes.

I wondered aloud to Allegra what might change if we told the story of her choice a little differently. Because we UFOAs have been so loyal for so long to a specific destination, we experience any deviation from the plan as a dramatic overhaul and even a sort of epic failure of our life as we knew it. Sometimes it really is an overhaul, but more often when we're making Directional decisions, it's actually just a slight recalibration of our route. Yes, it changes the possible outcomes and can be significant and life-altering, but it isn't necessarily the blowing up of our lives that we may perceive it to be.

Allegra's shift made complete sense to me. She was always all about the brain! The brain was always her direction. She thought her passion for the brain was going to be expressed through neurosurgery, but now she'd made a turn toward another brain-focused specialty, psychiatry. It's not as if everything she ever knew about herself and her interests was a sham. This was not a line in the sand where one version of her ended and another began. It was certainly not a failure. Rather, Allegra was evolving organically and Directionally, exactly as she was meant to. This was more like a small shift than a 180-degree turn.

There was a deeper shift that was also happening here, compounding the intensity of this choice. This wasn't just about a shift from neurosurgery to psychiatry or from any option A to any option B. It was also about a shift from the old Destinational way to the new Directional one, from being led by the Fear Self to being led by the True Self. *Of course* that's going to bring on complicated feelings! The path Allegra was convinced was the only one for her turned out not to be right for her after all. And as if that wasn't enough, she was also beginning to realize that the entire foundation of how she'd designed her life, the underlying premise of all her decision-making, hadn't been serving her and had actually been undermining her *this whole time*. That's jarring, to say the least.

Reassessing and transforming your approach to life and your life strategy is radical. This is not a small thing. And, as I frequently tell my clients, it often gets harder before it gets easier. This is not necessarily a sign that it's Directionally wrong. This can also be a sign that it's deep and lasting. We're playing the long game here. We're talking about building a life of inner ease, not one in which you avoid discomfort.

PS: Allegra chose psychiatry. And she loves it.

Your Fear Self vs. True Self Legend

Fill in the bottom section with your own information from your work in this chapter.

	Fear Self	True Self
Universal References		
Approach	Destinational	Directional
Goal	to survive	to thrive
Language	Four Omens; fear	nonverbal; alignment
Feels like	colder; hard and heavy; resistance	warmer; light and right; ease
Sounds like	words and justifications; logic	absence of verbal logic
Lives in	mind	body/sensations
Results in	blind ambition; unfulfillment; F-ache	aligned ambition; fulfillment; no F-ache
Your Personal References		
Name (if other than Fear/True Self)		
Reference/ shortcut	(e.g., Dr. Dick)	(e.g., Maine)
Your sensations	(e.g., ick)	(e.g., yay)

Phase III: Release

Letting Go of What's Holding You Back

So far, we've talked about using your Inner Navigation System to make aligned choices. But what happens if something out of alignment for you ends up in your life anyway, threatening to take you back toward Destinational thinking? Or when something that was once aligned no longer is? And what about all those legacy Fear Self, Directionally wrong decisions that are already in your life, keeping you stuck in your old Destinational default? How do we maintain a Directional Life once we've connected to it? Living Directionally is as much a process of making ongoing warmer, aligned decisions as it is a process of recognizing and eliminating those colder, misaligned parts of your life that jeopardize your hard-won Directional Life. This is the just-as-important flip side of trueing yourself and your life that clears the logjams from the Directional way and helps you stay the Directional course.

Sounds simple enough: add "Directionally right," get rid of "Directionally wrong." Boom. Done. Unfortunately, for us UFOAs, it tends not to be so straightforward.

Take my friend Virginia. For months, she had terrible headaches, which she claimed were manageable, dismissing them as "just" headaches. She treated them with increasing amounts of ibuprofen because, well, they were an inconvenient distraction from all that she was trying to accomplish as a mom and a corporate executive. Until, that is, she ended up in the ER, where she was diagnosed with what the doctor said was the worst sinus infection he'd ever seen. Incredulous, he asked her, "How are you walking around like that?"

When she first told me about this, I remember thinking that there was something familiar in her story. It was oddly parallel to my life at Google: I had never felt good, but I ignored the ill feeling for years. I sucked it up. I justified it, and I numbed it with every pain-management solution I could think of. I forced myself to get used to it . . . until it metastasized from something merely inconvenient into an emergency that couldn't *not* be addressed. In the meantime, I had settled for an impaired life. How *had* I been walking around like that?

This wasn't just a Virginia thing or a me thing. What Virginia was describing is how UFOAs walk around all day, every day. It's a consequence of Destinational Living; we're so focused on the destination that we either don't see or willfully ignore anything in the way, no matter how painful or obvious. Every UFOA I've worked with has had a whole bunch of "How are you walking around like thats," or HAYWALTs, as I began calling them. Think back to the question I asked myself on that office bathroom floor, the one most UFOAs ask themselves at some point: *How did I get here?* By tolerating HAYWALTs, that's how!

HAYWALTs are the misalignments that we convince ourselves aren't "that bad" and therefore ignore altogether, refusing to notice the pain and discomfort they cause. They're the poet Samuel Taylor Coleridge's proverbial albatrosses, hung about our necks, and we either pretend they aren't there or, worse, pretend we need them. *I truly like having this dead bird draped across my body, thank you very much.* With HAYWALTs, we gaslight *ourselves.*

You'll recognize HAYWALTs because they have a sandpapery quality to them; they chafe against the True Self, and they're uncomfortable, even painful, each and every time we interact with them. While we Underfulfilled Overachievers tend to be very familiar with these grating sandpaper sensations, we have no idea what's causing them or how to remedy them. And so we quietly assume that they must be part of standard operating procedure. In fact, we're just so damn used to being misaligned that we're typically not even consciously aware of their presence. That's what makes HAYWALTs so insidious.

Sure, we could just call them "misalignments" or "colder feelings" or "hard and heavies," but there is power in naming things precisely. HAYWALTs are such an impediment to successfully moving into alignment with ourselves, to living our most fulfilled lives, and to trueing ourselves that they require their own word—one that captures the particular UFOA psychology underpinning our typical tolerance of them. A HAYWALT is so much more than just "a thing I don't like."

I've seen in my practice over and over again that something shifts when we identify a thing as a HAYWALT by name. We become so much more likely to take it seriously, instead of continuing to justify it, deny it, or brush it off. There's an undeniably different flavor to saying "My job is a HAYWALT" rather than just "I don't like my job." Implicit in our labeling something a HAYWALT is ownership, accountability, and, ultimately, action.

One of my all-time favorite examples of the life-changing nature of HAYWALT identification didn't even come from a client of mine;

it came from a friend of a client. Grace dropped out of college for financial reasons and took a full-time job. She is a beautiful writer and was able to build a thriving copywriting career that she enjoyed, but it nagged her that she hadn't finished college and didn't have a degree. For years, she shrugged it off, barely acknowledging it, even to herself. Clearly, it wasn't essential to her livelihood; she was in a great place in her career and in her life. And then my client told her about the concept of the HAYWALT. As Grace tells it, this was a revelation. Immediately, she knew that her incomplete college degree was a HAYWALT for her, and once she'd identified it as such, it became an undeniable priority in a way that just "I wish I'd graduated from college" had not. With the HAYWALT label comes a mandate to address it. For her, the naming alone was empowering and galvanizing. Soon after, she did in fact make a plan to complete her degree, and once she did, she reported feeling so much lighter and freer and more herself. She told me that she'd had no idea how much it had been weighing her down.

How was Virginia able to disregard the pain she was in for so long? Why did Grace ignore her desire to complete her college degree? What made it possible for me to tolerate my misery at Google? A lifetime of sandpaper living, a lifetime of being conditioned to tolerate pain and discomfort in order to stay the Destinational course, a lifetime of the ingrained belief that being a responsible adult means accepting a whole bunch of crap and sacrificing our wants and needs and our own comfort, for "success" and the comfort of others. So deep is this patterning for UFOAs that any internal sense of suffering, regardless of its variety, simply doesn't register as being worthy of, or requiring of, a response. It barely enters our consciousness as valid information at all!

HAYWALTs are essentially lies we're consciously or unconsciously telling ourselves. Eliminating them is about dismantling those lies. We can't true ourselves while also maintaining the things that knocked us out of alignment in the first place. We can't dismantle the old Destinational Living patterns while also upholding the HAYWALT infrastructure that keeps them in place. We have to start learning how to tell ourselves the truth, because we often don't even know we're not! Incredibly, this is not something we've been taught to do. At its core, identifying HAYWALTs—and, really, the entirety of UFOA recovery—is an exercise in telling yourself the truth about your life.

What comes to mind when you think of tolerating HAYWALTs? Google had been my biggest HAYWALT, but that was certainly not the extent of it. Living in San Francisco was a HAYWALT for me. I've stayed in relationships that had become HAYWALTs. I've hired people who weren't good fits for my team and so became HAYWALTs. I've definitely committed to exercise routines that turned into HAYWALTs.

Whether you have agreed to give a keynote that you don't want to give, or are staying in a relationship that doesn't make you feel good, or are pursuing a career that makes you shrivel inside, you're participating in your own misalignment and the dismissal of your True Self. And the result will always be the same: unfulfillment. You simply cannot live a fulfilled, authentic Directional Life if it is filled with HAYWALTs.

DeHAYWALTing, therefore, is the process by which we both rid ourselves of what we no longer want in our lives and make space for what we do want. There's an opportunity cost to everything, and HAYWALTs, especially, take up a lot of space. If we're saying yes to a HAYWALT, we're inherently saying no to a potential Directionally right opportunity. HAYWALTs are drags on our fulfillment and alignment—not only in and of themselves, but also in how they block us from being able to add in anything of the Something Bigger, Directionally right variety.

Our task in this phase isn't so much to find our alignment and fulfillment as it is to address all the things that are blocking us from accessing them. In other words, we must deHAYWALT our lives. Only then will our Directional Lives have enough space to unfold.

The DeHAYWALTing Process

The deHAYWALTing process is like a spring cleaning of your life. We'll approach upgrading your life just as we might approach upgrading your closet. There are three steps: (1) inventorying and identifying what needs to go, (2) sorting, and (3) eliminating.

If you've ever read Marie Kondo's book *The Life-Changing Magic of Tidying Up* or watched the Netflix spin-off, you already have a sense of what this process is like. Your first step is a Kondo-esque process of removing all the items in the "closet" of your life, taking them off the hangers, and laying them all out. You're going to "try on" every single item and ask, "Is this aligned, or is this a HAY-WALT?" (That's our equivalent to Kondo's "Does it spark joy?") If it's aligned, it can go back into the closet of your life. If it's not, it goes straight onto the HAYWALT pile. In other words, if it's not a "Hell yes," as the saying goes, then it's a "Hell no."

HAYWALT identification relies on your trued Inner Navigation System. When you try on a HAYWALT, it will feel like the colder, Directionally wrong, hard-and-heavy Fear Self side of the spectrum, whereas inhabiting something aligned feels like—you guessed it— the warmer, Directionally right, light-and-right True Self side. Go back and check your personal INS legend for a reminder. But here you're not moving yourself toward where you want to go so much as you are learning how to see what keeps you from going there.

Let's start with your calendar. Imagine you've gone through and listed out each entry for the next month—client meetings, all-hands meeting on the tenth, team off-site, lunch date with Deb, Pilates class every Monday and Thursday, local mutual aid meeting, meetup with financial adviser, concert date, niece's dance recital, prescription pickup at drugstore, and so on. One of the items on your list is an upcoming ski weekend. You try it on, assuming it's aligned—it is, after all, a vacation! But as you let it settle in your body and ask, "Is this aligned?" feeling within for the sensations you know indicate "alignment"—warmth, lightness and rightness, ease, freedom, relief—you are surprised to discover that what you actually feel is more aptly encapsulated by the words *ugh, ick, hard and heavy, anxious,* and *clenched.* Your ski trip is actually a HAYWALT.

You had no idea that you didn't really want to go on this trip. You reflect a little more and admit that you hate sharing a house with other people. You actually don't even like skiing. It's more money than you wanted to spend, and you'd much rather be on a beach somewhere. The whole thing just sounds exhausting.

What now? Your first UFOA reaction might be to ignore the bad feeling, to pretend it's aligned because it "should" be aligned, and to put it neatly back into the closet of your life. *No one will know, right?! It's not that big of a deal. How bad could it be?* This sounds a lot like *I'll just take some Advil and get over it.* And yet it's hugely important that you do not ignore it. Tell yourself the truth.

There are many reasons why you may resist. There's the desire to please others and the guilt of disrupting everyone's plans. *My friends and partner would be so disappointed,* you might think. And there's the fact that you want to be seen as easygoing and chill, not as a whiner or a complainer. You don't want to appear entitled or ungrateful. UFOAs tend to believe that being easygoing and "flexible"—making one's own needs and preferences secondary to everyone else's—is generous, the "right" thing to do, and a prerequisite for earning love. Being "chill" and "up for anything" feels much safer than being something that could be construed as disruptive. You believe that would jeopardize the relationships that matter to you.

Sometimes there's a fear that if you eliminate the HAYWALT, you'll be left with an unfillable void. *What if I don't make any other plans that weekend? What am I going to do? Sit at home and doomscroll?!* If you don't go on the ski trip, there's a chance you'll have no vacation at all. Or you might worry that if you leave your HAYWALT-y relationship, you'll be single and lonely forever. What if you quit that toxic job and then no one ever wants to hire you again and you're left jobless for the rest of time? (This is scarcity thinking, a classic Fear Self tactic.) The status quo–preserving Fear Self will always choose the bird-in-hand logic that goes, "The misery you know is better than the possibilities you don't."

But here are the questions I want to amplify for you instead: Why the hell would you spend your time and money and vacation days to go on a trip that you don't want to go on? Why go on a vacation that is going to leave you more depleted than recharged? To what end? So that a few people aren't disappointed? When it's articulated this way, we can clearly see the mental gymnastics we go through to convince ourselves to do something we actually don't want to do.

All of these concerns—disappointing others, being difficult and disruptive, falling into a dark, lonely void—are fears that get in the way of calling a HAYWALT a HAYWALT. But I've found that the biggest barrier to identifying HAYWALTs is believing we have to know exactly how to address them in order to safely identify them. We tend to skip ahead to "fixing" the problem before we've even named it—I see you, Destinational thinking! Our willingness to define something as a HAYWALT becomes dependent on our current ability to know how to solve it.

Honest appraisal of HAYWALTs gets a lot easier when you know this: you do not have to *do* anything about the HAYWALTs once you discover them. Right now, this is a yes-or-no and multiple-choice exercise, not a problem-solving one. This ski trip is choice B, HAYWALT. What you decide to do with that admission, what events may or may not transpire as a result, what conversations may or may not take place, and any other future forecasting your mind is tempted to do are all irrelevant at this stage of deHAYWALTing.

This is key: we need to detach identification from elimination in order to tell ourselves the truth about our lives. These comprise two different steps of this process for a reason. For now, just keep coming back to *Is it aligned, or is it a HAYWALT?* That's all you need to know. Acknowledging and identifying HAYWALTs is incredibly powerful in and of itself and can lead to significant shifts, even if you know there's no immediate recourse. I would rather you say, "This ski trip is a HAYWALT, and I'm going on it anyway," than have you lie to yourself and tell everyone that you're thrilled to be going. HAYWALTs compound, so we want to get in the habit of correctly and promptly naming them.

A ski trip is far from the biggest or most invasive HAYWALT out there, and quite a privileged one at that, and yet the mechanism and the pattern are exactly the same whether it's a weekend vacation, a career path, a marriage, a friendship, a course of study, or an addiction.

To identify something as a HAYWALT is simply to say, "This doesn't feel Directionally right." And then, eventually, hopefully: "I'm no longer willing to walk around like that."

YOUR TURN: DEHAYWALTING WITH THE CALENDAR PURGE

Your calendar is a great catalog of "receipts" of the people, places, and things that you choose to have in your life, and therefore it's the perfect place to begin inventorying the "closet" of your life. Treat every calendar entry, both personal and professional, as if it were an item of clothing in that closet. In your mind, "try on" every single coffee date, meeting, meal, work project, and social gathering. *Is this aligned, or is this a HAYWALT?*

Imagine being there or how you'll feel when you wake up that morning knowing that this thing is on your schedule. Notice every time you have an "ugh" reaction. Pay attention when it's something you tend to try to wiggle out of at the last minute. If you get a queasy feeling in your stomach or a tightness in your chest or throat, that's undoubtedly a feeling of "colder" and "hard and heavy." That's a HAYWALT.

Before we get started, I have three tips to keep in mind. First, nothing is too big or too small. Whether it's your entire field of work or just something to do with PowerPoint decks, both are totally legit HAYWALTs. A HAYWALT could be that fitness instructor whom everyone else seems to worship but whom you find plain annoying. If it goes against your own INS, then it's a HAYWALT. Maybe everything foundational in your life is a HAYWALT. That's how it was for me. My relationship, my job, my office, the city I lived in—all were HAYWALTs at one point. Remember, you don't need to know how to "fix" them in order to declare them.

Second, no justifying allowed! There's no taking out a dress that's too small, that you wore when you were sixteen, and telling yourself, *Well, maybe if I took it to the tailor . . . or if it was the right temperature and I was on vacation in a beach town, I might wear it.* Or: *It's just one weekend.* Or: *It's easy money and looks good on my résumé.* None of that. The unofficial tagline of deHAYWALTing is the saying "If it's not a 'Hell yes,' then it's a 'Hell no.'" One client told me that the voice she hears when she's narrating her own deHAYWALTing process—for all you millennials out there—is Heidi Klum's signature staccato on *Project Runway*: "You're either in or you're out."

And, third, HAYWALTs are subjective. There's no ultimate truth about what is a HAYWALT and what is not—after all, that would be Destinational Living and the Omen of Objectivity! There's no right and wrong. No judgments in this. DeHAYWALTing is a wholly personal process that's particular to you and no one else. I've had clients for whom being single and longing for love was a major HAYWALT in their lives. I've also had clients who were beset by the exact opposite HAYWALT: being partnered and really wanting to be single.

Step One: Identifying Your HAYWALTs

Let's begin!

1. Pull up your calendar(s) and comb through at least the last thirty days and next thirty days of your work and personal commitments. Make a list of every item or type of item that you find.

2. "Try on" each item one by one; determine whether it's "aligned" or a HAYWALT.

3. On your list, put a check mark next to everything that is warmer and aligned and an X next to every item that is colder and a HAYWALT.

Congratulations! This is the beginning of your HAYWALT list. Don't worry about doing anything except identifying them at this point, and don't judge whether it is right/wrong or good/bad to have these particular HAYWALTs.

Here are some examples of calendar items that may be HAY-WALTs: the conference in Vegas that you attended last month, coffee with a frenemy, every meeting before eight o'clock in the morning, every meeting with *that* client, every project with *that* VP, every day that you don't take a lunch break, Tuesdays, that one dinner party, anything on Saturday that involves real clothes, commuting, Zoom, "pick your brain" meetings.

Step Two: Sorting Your HAYWALTs

The next step is to take all the HAYWALTs you just identified and prepare them for the elimination phase. To do this, divide them into three lists (or "piles"), just as you would clothing in a closet purge:

1. Remove

2. Maybe

3. Keep Anyway

When deciding the pile to which each HAYWALT gets assigned, we are not expecting a perfect and immediate identify-and-release cycle. Ideally, of course, we'd notice a HAYWALT, and we get rid of it. But because we're human (often a shock to UFOAs!) and up against some major Destinational legacy stuff, this is bound to activate some Fear Self reactions and is often hard, emotional work, not quick work. We want to give ourselves a deHAYWALTing process that actually sets us up for success. Take your time with deHAYWALTing. These three lists create a bit of space for us between identifying HAYWALTs and eliminating them, which takes some of the pressure off and ultimately leads to more effective deHAYWALTing.

The first list, the Remove pile, is where we want to put as many of our HAYWALTs as possible. These are the ones you are sure are HAYWALTs; you're more than ready to be done with them. They're on their way to Goodwill, and you're never going to think about them again after today.

It can also be useful to think of these, especially the bigger ones, as HAYWALTs that you are "donating" to someone else for whom they will be in alignment. Leaving a job that is a HAYWALT for you is really donating it or making it available to someone else for whom that job has been a long-held dream and for whom it is truly aligned. The same goes for a relationship—release a HAYWALT-y partner so that they, and you, can connect with someone else who is a "Hell yes."

Next, there are the Maybes. These are the things that sound like *I didn't see it before, but now I can see why I might need to get rid of this. I'm not sure how. I don't know if I'm quite ready. I need to sleep on it. I need to give myself some time to adjust to this idea.* Perhaps your apartment is a maybe. Perhaps you've been trying to love your apartment, and through this process, you can finally say, "This apartment just doesn't suit me anymore. I want more space in a more affordable neighborhood that's not as close to the subway, since I now work from home most of the time." That might be a lot to swallow at this moment, though. Moving is a big deal. It's hard to make a call in one fell swoop and just say, "Yep, I'm moving. Going for it." Some processing time may be in order to decide when and if a move is possible.

Lastly, and hopefully the smallest of the piles, is the Keep Anyway pile. Let's be clear: this contains things that are still HAYWALTs—things that we *know* are not serving us—but we just can't fathom getting rid of them (yet!), for whatever reasons. These HAYWALTS are usually those that have very deep roots. For example, there were many years when Google went on my Keep Anyway list. Of course, I didn't have this language for it then, but I knew it wasn't filling me up. I just wasn't ready to consider the possibility that it could be eliminated or donated to someone else. I didn't yet have the courage I needed to toss it onto the Get the Hell Out of My Life pile.

There's no shame in this category. Again, I would much rather you have a HAYWALT named and living in this pile of "HAYWALTs I choose to tolerate and therefore continue participating in my own suffering" (just kidding, but not really!) than a HAYWALT that you pretend isn't actually a HAYWALT. Allowing HAYWALTs to remain hanging in the unconscious is way more dangerous to Directional Living than acknowledging them while still continuing to live with them.

Step Three: Elimination, or DeHAYWALTing

Imagine for a moment that all the HAYWALTs on your three lists get addressed. Each and every one of them, disappeared. Don't worry for a second about how that happens; just go down your lists and try to immerse yourself in what it would feel like to knock all of them out of your life. What would it feel like to be 100 percent HAYWALT-free? Imagine how different your life would be—how much lighter, how much more spacious, and how much less encumbered—without these HAYWALTs.

Imagine a state in which there is nothing in your life that you are tolerating unnecessarily or unconsciously. Unmanageable client load—gone! Texts from your boss over the weekend—gone! Your kids' impossible picky-eating phase—gone! Prohibitive back pain from an old injury—gone! Subway commute—done! Misogynistic micro-aggressions at work—good riddance! Invisible labor and lopsided household chores at home—goodbye! Hustle culture—so long!

Envision a world in which no aspect of your work, relationships, or family life is a HAYWALT. When you look at your calendar, not a single thing makes you recoil with dread. To the contrary, it's filled with things that you're excited about attending. Your life starts to feel less like a slog. Instead, there is eager anticipation and curiosity for all that is unfolding. *What will alignment bring me today? What new experiences are upcoming on my Directionally right path?* When there are no HAYWALTs standing between you and your Directionally right course, keeping you tethered to your "shoulds" and Destinational defaults, your INS becomes less staticky and easier to hear. Your Directionally right path becomes clear. This may sound like a fairy tale to you at this point, but it's not an exaggeration. I assure you that this is what you have to look forward to at the end of our work together. What a relief!

While a 100 percent HAYWALT-free life isn't realistic for most of us—especially in a world where some of our biggest HAYWALTs are systemic and structural—experiencing drastically more of this freedom is. You are not a failure by any means if you continue to live with some HAYWALTs. Embarking on your personal deHAYWALT-ing endeavor is still worth it. In fact, it's essential to UFOA recovery.

Of course, HAYWALTs don't just disappear (sadly). It takes some work on our part, which brings us to the main event, the actual elimination. This is where you figure out how to address the HAY-WALTs that you're ready to let go of. Don't get overwhelmed! You don't have to do it all at once, and I have extra strategies for you in the back of the book, too, to help.

DeHAYWALTing is course correction. At some point, we got out of alignment and off track, and this is the process of rerouting. What we're doing with HAYWALT removal is troubleshooting the "warmest" way to reroute back into Directionally right, trued alignment. DeHAYWALTing, therefore, will always feel warmer than living with the HAYWALTs. The "Go where it's warm" mantra leads this process. Let our magic questions—*Where is the freedom?* and *Where is the relief?*—be your guide. Only we're not just asking where the freedom and relief are; we're also asking: *What is the smallest action I can take to find freedom and relief?*

The first and crucial step of elimination is to identify the HAY-WALT precisely. You'll want to be as specific as possible at this stage so that you don't eliminate more, or less, than is necessary for alignment. You want to make sure that you're solving the right problem, not just blowing things up. For instance, just because there's something HAYWALT-y about your relationship doesn't mean that the whole relationship is automatically a HAYWALT. We don't all need to quit our jobs, get divorced, and sell our homes. Maybe less drastic modifications would sufficiently deHAYWALT these situations, such as ending a contract with a specific client, coming to new agreements about household responsibilities, or just rearranging the furniture. On the other hand, you don't want to stick around making incremental changes to your work life and your family relationships and your furniture if the HAYWALT really is much bigger.

Returning for a moment to our ski vacation example, at first you may have only known that the trip was a HAYWALT and gave you the icks. But you don't want to overreach and cancel if it turns out that the HAYWALT is just the activity of skiing itself; maybe going on a vacation with friends feels Directionally right—you just want to spend your time doing a more aligned activity while you're there, drinking hot chocolate in the lodge, or snowshoeing perhaps. You also don't want to underestimate the HAYWALT and plan another vacation with this same group of people if the HAYWALT really is this entire group and the aligned action is to stop socializing with them, period. It matters enormously what, precisely, makes something a HAYWALT for you.

Perhaps you're going through your lists, and you know something about your job is HAYWALT-y, but you just wrote "Work." You're going to want to dig in there and get specific about the HAYWALT. Is it your entire industry? Or is it just your particular company (i.e., taking a similar role at a different company with a more aligned culture would enable you to deHAYWALT adequately)? Or could an internal transfer to a new role, a new team, or a new manager at the same company be the warmer solution?

One client of mine was a well-known and successful psychotherapist who managed her own group practice. This had been her longtime dream, and yet she was miserable. She came to me fully prepared to leave psychotherapy altogether. She planned to hand her practice over to a colleague and start the hard process of seeking a new career. Once we dug in together, however, we found that the HAYWALT wasn't being a therapist; it was working in therapeutic areas that didn't light her up. She'd been working with anyone on anything when what she was so passionate about was working with new moms. Recasting her practice and specializing in the area where she felt most invigorated and inspired deHAYWALTed the situation. Sometimes the smallest sufficient action does indeed mean dramatically changing your life, but often, something significantly less extreme is all that is necessary. Again, this will require radical honesty with yourself. No one else can know your HAYWALTs with the precision you can.

It's also true that you sometimes might not have enough information to be precise quite yet. That's okay. For example, you might need to test out working from home full-time to see if that's warmer and meaningfully changes your experience with your job. It can take time to know whether changing the dynamic of a friendship will suffice or whether you really do need to distance yourself from that friend entirely. And, of course, you can explore all of your HAYWALTs Directionally! Test and learn here. Get curious and investigate. Start with the smallest action that offers some relief or a sense of "warmer"—only taking on new psychotherapy clients that you can't wait to work with, modifying the vacation instead of ditching the friend group, transferring teams internally—and expand from there until you can be precise.

Now, back to your lists. It's unlikely that you'll be able to address every HAYWALT at once. Pick five low-hanging fruits from the Remove pile and commit to eliminating them ASAP. These might be things like pausing your subscription to *The New Yorker*, which just keeps piling up unread; ditching the HIIT classes you hate; finally getting the dishwasher fixed; and RSVPing "No" to that thing you really don't want to attend. This will get you into a deHAYWALT-ing rhythm and build some momentum. Most importantly, you'll start to feel a sense of relief and spaciousness, which is by far the best motivator to keep going.

You'll also want to pick five from the second pile—things that you're ready to release but that you may need a little more time to sort. Commit to eliminating those HAYWALTs within a month or two. Put this deadline on your calendar! These might entail some difficult conversations and more complex problem-solving. (See the strategies at the end of the book.)

List your ten selected HAYWALTs below, get as precise as you can in defining them, and then brainstorm the most aligned deHAYWALTing action. Finally, list the deHAYWALTing action that you're committing to.

First Round of DeHAYWALTing

Original HAYWALT	precise HAYWALT	deHAYWALT action
Example: therapy practice	*no specialty*	*specialize in new moms*
1.		
2.		
3.		
4.		
5.		

Second Round of DeHAYWALTing

1.

2.

3.

4.

5.

Now, don't go out and acquire a ton of new HAYWALTs to take the place of the old ones! The goal is only to add in well-fitting items of clothing aligned with your revamped Directional style. Ideally, over time, you'll move through your lists until you've cleared out all your legacy HAYWALTs. Then, as you move increasingly toward your Directionally right, you'll add fewer and fewer HAYWALTs— and when you do, or when things that weren't HAYWALTs in the past become HAYWALTs in the present, you'll quickly recognize and address them. The more Directionally right your life is, the fewer HAYWALTs you'll have. Eventually, you'll become so adept at recognizing HAYWALTs that you'll address them before they have time to settle into your life. This way, you won't ever have to do a full HAYWALT purge again. The fewer HAYWALTs you have, the lower your tolerance for them will be, and the more motivated you'll become to eliminate them.

Phase IV: Orient

Finding Your Big Direction

I f you're uncomfortable, even terrified, at this point, that's okay. You're not doing it wrong, I promise. You've just landed at the line-in-the-sand moment of your transition from Destinational to Directional Living, when what once existed no longer does but before anything new has been created or is even fathomable. It's the darkest-before-the-dawn moment, after the dissolution but before the transformation. You've now cut loose a lot of crusty old Destinational stuff, and this may have left you with what feels like a gaping void. You may have no idea what's next or how to fill it. This juncture of uncertainty can be intimidating and disorienting and can leave you grief-stricken. Still, keep going. Because this moment is also steeped in potential—in freedom.

There's an expression, "the breakdown is the breakthrough," and there's perhaps no better way to describe what many UFOAs experience at this stage. For most of us UFOAs, the "breakdown" side of this equation feels like everything we've been trying to avoid our whole lives—the appearance of incompetence and imperfection, of falling apart, of not knowing where we're going. But these feelings of discomfort and dread, even doom, that we associate with a breakdown are often indistinguishable from the feelings of a break-*through*. You can't have the breakthrough—the new Directional Life of fulfillment—without the breakdown—of your old Destinational Life.

Imagine what is possible from here, what you can build and create when you're in full alignment and in full expression of your True Self. Imagine what it would feel like to find work that doesn't feel like "work," to stop living from vacation to vacation, to look forward to Monday as much as Friday, and to wake up every morning (okay, most mornings) and think, *I am doing exactly what I am meant to be doing*. Imagine what it would be like if decisions, in all aspects of your life, felt like opportunities to advance the thrilling plot of your life's story. Imagine how it would feel to be able to make those decisions with ease and clarity. Imagine how much of a relief it would be to stop feeling like an impostor and to see your F-ache disappear. This is what awaits you on the other side of the breakdown.

The Big Direction

In these next phases, you will set out on the Directional road trip of the rest of your life. You'll start to navigate through each leg of your trip using your Inner Navigation System to take aligned action, iterating toward what I call your Big Direction.

Even though you're making the whole trip with just the illumination of the single next right step, it still helps to have a sense of the broad strokes, high-level Big Direction, even and especially when it's dark, and that's what we'll be working on developing in this phase.

A Big Direction can feel dangerously close to a Destination. The distinction between a Big Direction and a Destination—between perhaps west as a direction and the West Coast as a destination—is how we are using it: as something we orient *toward* versus something we are attached to. It's a beacon versus a goal. A destination is somewhere we are committed to arriving—it's the whole point of the trip. If your destination is the West Coast, anywhere other than the West Coast is unacceptable. If you're set on the West Coast and you wake up in Colorado, say, you'd be annoyed and confused at the least, and probably perseverate on where you went wrong and how you could have screwed up the trip so badly. You'd consider this trip a big, fat failure. If your *direction* is west, or toward the West Coast, though, and you land in Colorado when coming from New York, and you absolutely adore it there, then the West Coast has perfectly served its purpose. You'd consider the trip a great success!

For a real-life example, AOC's Big Direction was public service, whereas becoming a congresswoman was a Directionally right step along the way. (It remains to be seen what her next iteration will be!) Neither public service nor congresswoman, however, was an intended Destination at the outset. My Big Direction was counseling or consulting of some sort, but becoming a coach was an aligned iteration of that Big Direction. Writing this book is another iteration. Again, none of these things—counseling/consulting, coaching, or writing a book—was a predetermined Destination.

If the concept of Big Direction still seems contradictory to "just the headlights," stay with me. Your Big Direction is the crucial difference between what we're doing with Directional Living and wandering. There's nothing wrong with wandering. Big fan of wandering over here. We don't do it nearly enough! In fact, sometimes that's the best, or the only, course of action, especially when you're starting out. I also happen to believe that you will get to where you're going if you only ever wander, as long as you are following your Inner

Navigation System. But the point is that it's not necessary to do so. With Directional Living, we don't need to occupy a state of permanent wandering, and certainly not of aimless drifting.

I suggest thinking about Directional Living like the scientific method for your life where your Big Direction is your hypothesis. The difference between orienting toward a Big Direction and wandering is the same idea as conducting scientific research with and without a hypothesis. You may indeed end up stumbling upon penicillin by getting up every day and tinkering in a lab with no hypothesis, but it's more likely, more efficient, and more reliable if you have the guiding principle of a hypothesis you're testing. Not to mention the fact that we do usually have some sense of what we want to explore. Most scientists don't begin experimenting because they want to discover anything about anything; they're interested in black holes or cancer genes or the reproductive habits of vampire squid. There's some sort of inclination toward an area of focus, no matter how broad it may be.

Or let's revisit the original context of the Doctorow quotation: writing a novel. You may begin work on a novel by writing a bunch of disparate scenes that seemingly have nothing to do with one another in order to get going. Most likely, however, at some point, you will begin to have a sense of what you suspect your book will be about and who the characters are, whether the genre is sci-fi or romance, or it's narrated by a baroness or a cat, even if you don't know exactly how the plot will unfold. Certainly, your hypothesis of what your book is about will evolve as you write, but it doesn't remain in a black box until you're done writing.

So, why cultivate a Big Direction? The first reason is that your curiosity will tend to coalesce around some themes, if not now, then eventually. This will happen organically, but there are also ways that we can nurture this vision. We need not ignore these patterns when they arise, especially because they can help us better tolerate the uncertainty of navigating life that Directional Living asks us to acknowledge. We just need to be conscious of how we hold these patterns—loosely like a Directional hypothesis that orients us instead of rigidly like a Destination that we're chained to.

The second reason is that it's supremely helpful for our UFOA brains to have some semblance of structure for our lives, some connective tissue that helps us to articulate our own evolving story to ourselves. Living with the uncertainty of not having a definitive destination from which to reverse engineer our infallible life plan is a huge leap for our outdated UFOA operating systems. It's the difference between "I have no idea where I'm going" and "I have a sense of where I'm going, though I don't have an exact destination." It seems subtle, but the lived experience between these two statements is drastically different. So, we might as well take advantage of this scaffolding as it emerges.

Lastly, one thing we do know is that "purpose" is foundational to fulfillment. Psychology research shows that being connected to "something bigger" than yourself—certainly "something bigger" than your to-do list—is linked with psychological well-being and resilience. It's a key component, if not *the* key, to a meaningful and fulfilling life. In Directional Living, your Big Direction serves a similar function to what "life purpose" might, but there's an important distinction that we need to make. "Purpose" has been framed for us UFOAs (you'll be shocked to know) in a manner that is so misleading and harmful that it has actually had the effect of keeping us from feeling "purposeful" in what we do. Perhaps even just seeing the word *purpose* here makes you cringe. What happens if I tell you that you need to identify your one life purpose that will determine the rest of your life, right now, before you can go any further? Do you feel inspired? Motivated? Energized? Probably not. You likely feel intimidated and stressed. If you're like most UFOAs, you start short-circuiting. You panic, scrambling for an answer that isn't there, and blow a fuse. Your mind might go blank. As a result, you do nothing. Or maybe you make up something arbitrary. Also ineffective! The very thing that is supposed to be motivating you is holding you back. Forget your purpose.

In the Destinational world order, we are sold a distorted ideal of a grand "life purpose"—it's something to achieve, another box to check, another tool to demonstrate our worth. Destinational thinking teaches that it's our singular and sacred duty to identify said purpose before we can *really* begin living. And then, of course, it festers into another thing at which we fail—we fail to find our purpose, which means we fail to move forward. Until we find this "life purpose," we remain stuck, spinning our wheels, distracted, while we persist in searching. "Life purpose" becomes just a sexy, soulful spin on the classic strategy of Destinational achievement. Take the same old success narrative but make it destiny. Otherwise, as this "life purpose" narrative goes, you're wasting your time and your life.

This is a UFOA trap, not a truth. True Purpose is not a destination. It's not a goal, or a title, or a place at which you arrive. It's not a fixed and finite thing that you "find" once and for all and then need to hold on to for dear life lest you lose it. Nor do you "have" a purpose, as if it's a possession, that you either acquire or don't acquire. And it's certainly not something you owe other people to justify your existence on Earth.

Purpose is—yep, you guessed it—a direction, not a destination. It's your inner sense of aligned ambition, not blind ambition for an observable outcome. You don't *achieve* purpose; you move *toward* it. It's not a specific point on a map; it's a way of being—of being aligned, of being *on* purpose. Purpose acts like a verb—something you're becoming rather than somewhere or something you are. And it's not precious or narrow or precarious, like walking on a tightrope, where you could stumble and lose it at any moment. It's alive and expansive.

The term *purpose* has become so coded and loaded with Destinationalism's achievement narratives that it has lost its effectiveness. It's hard for most UFOAs to separate it from Destinational Living. As a result, I've mostly stopped using the word altogether. Instead, I use the terms *Big Direction* and *Something Bigger* to refer to *Directional* "purpose." Your Something Bigger is your most Directionally right, most aligned Big Direction. It's sometimes referred to as your North Star, the true north to which your Inner Navigation System is calibrated.

I like these terms because they're open and loose and unspecific and give us a lot more space in which to move around and evolve and experiment. They offer a roomy container for living Directionally, not a narrow point. *Something Bigger* and *Big Direction* invite us to be undefined and flexible without feeling aimless. They provide just the right amount of structure.

With your Big Direction life hypothesis, we're going for a broad, best-guess theory of the truest, most aligned path forward within an aspect of your life and we'll be walking through the process for finding it together. As with any scientifically sound experiment, it's not about getting it "right" or accurately predicting the outcome; it's only about getting it *Directionally* right. That's so much less pressure! You have your "headlights" in the form of your calibrated and trued Inner Navigation System, which you use to make specific aligned decisions. Now you can use that same INS guidance to inform your most aligned Big Direction hypothesis. It's just another game of warmer-colder and of following your curiosity.

By the end of this chapter, you'll be orienting toward your Something Bigger hypothesis, and you'll be ready to test and learn, collecting data through your lived experiences, iterating, and refining that Big Direction as you go. Your Something Bigger direction will change and evolve, as you do and as the world does.

Lyla and the Purpose UFOAs

"I lost my purpose," my new client Lyla whispered, ashamed, at our first meeting, even though we were alone. "If I even ever had it."

Lyla was pretty much *the* expert on all things community: building and scaling engaged communities, IRL and online. She'd done it for coworking spaces, for tech companies, for online support groups, for education services, for political campaigns, for nonprofits, for movements. It's something she'd always known how to do intuitively. In high school, she was the class president and had started a conversation about "intentionally designing the culture" that the student body wanted to see on campus. It was far-fetched at the time, and yet it worked; things changed. In college, various groups on campus—from the film society and the Spoken Word Collective to the social clubs and the Alliance for Social Justice—noticed Lyla's talents and enlisted her to help them attract and engage new members. She'd had a side hustle since before she even knew that was a thing. She'd gone on to work at a tech start-up, where she built an app for online-to-IRL community building that was hugely successful and eventually acquired. After that, she was an early hire at a coworking space, where she was offered a position as the director of community.

But then, she had started getting restless. She thought that maybe she just needed a new challenge. Maybe she wasn't "leaning in" to her "growth edge" hard enough. So she decided to "pivot," as she was advised to do, and she transitioned into running her own community-design consultancy and advisory. This worked for a while. She got to pick her clients, touch more and different kinds of communities, and make a broader impact and contribution. Her influence grew. It seemed like she was being interviewed on a new podcast every week. Maybe she just needed to do more things! Eventually, she launched her own digital course and built a thriving online business as well. She even added "professor" to her multihyphenate career after a business school in New York City recruited her to teach a community-building-in-business course. She sat on the boards of multiple for-profit and nonprofit organizations. No day was the same. Her work was varied, and her career growth appeared unstoppable. She'd thought it was The Thing—the great work of her life. She had a personal mission statement and everything. She was good at this work—great, even. She'd done everything right. And yet. There it was again, that quintessential UFOA phrase: "I had a great-on-paper life, *and yet . . .*"

Lyla was a newer iteration of UFOA, one I'd been starting to see more of: people whose lives look good on paper not only because they're successful, financially or in terms of influence, but also because they are doing something that seems to *matter*.

The classic UFOA isn't so concerned with "purpose" or meaning, because they've been taught that the achievement of success is *inherently* meaningful and fulfilling. They don't initially bother asking, "What is my purpose?" And it typically isn't until the Fulfillment Ache gets bad enough that their lack of any semblance of "purpose" dawns on them.

But Lyla and her Purpose UFOA peers were coming to me with not only great-on-paper lives that didn't feel so great but also the additional pressure and imperative of a "calling." These Purpose UFOAs had done everything right and checked all the boxes (now including a shiny new "find life purpose" box), but they were still miserable, unfulfilled, and more confused than ever. They were doing work as executive directors at nonprofits, as college professors, as directors of "corporate social responsibility" and "diversity, equity, and inclusion," as CMOs for social entrepreneurship organizations, as journalists—work they thought would offer not only success but also a sense of meaning. They believed that so long as their work seemed important to the world, then it would seem important to them, too . . . *right?*

Adding "purpose" to the equation doesn't change the result. Achievement plus "purpose" still equals Destinational Success. Their UFOA programming wasn't just saying that the accumulation of achievements would keep them safe and bestow fulfillment upon them; it was also saying that they must additionally "find (and achieve) their purpose" in order to live a safe and happy life.

It's even easier to be convinced that the problem is *you* when you're doing "important" and "meaningful" things, and easier still to be convinced that you should only work harder and produce more things that "matter." This supposedly liberating notion of "life purpose" had become another Destinational deceit for UFOAs. This was not helping them make the most of their "one wild and precious life," as many a Purpose UFOA often quoted to me. It was doing the opposite. I suspect this is not what this quote's author, Mary Oliver, had in mind.

In Lyla's case, what she was doing looked, on the surface, like it "should" be full of purpose and meaning, not only because she was "successful" but also because it was about bringing people together. How could that *not* be fulfilling?! Lyla recounted how people were constantly telling her that they were jealous she had found her purpose and had been able to turn it into a successful career "on her own terms." She was even regularly invited onto podcasts and panels to talk specifically about her successful and amazing purpose-driven career!

But, as we've learned, looking like you're doing something that matters and feeling like you're doing something that matters *to you* are two entirely different things. Not even meaningful impacts that are changing people's lives can mask misalignment and separation from the True Self.

I assured Lyla that this was nothing to be ashamed of and that she was far from alone—in fact, she was a cutting-edge, burgeoning new kind of UFOA. But first, we needed to clarify why she thought it was so important to find this "life purpose" and what, exactly, she thought "having it" would do for her.

She looked confused and responded as almost every Purpose UFOA does: "Isn't purpose the cure for unfulfillment?"

"Finding your purpose" isn't the cure for unfulfillment. *Directional Living* is the cure for unfulfillment. And that most often starts with your Big Direction. So as I told my workshop group many years ago, the assignment—for Lyla and for you—is to *forget your purpose*. That is, forget the chokehold of the purpose imperative with which most UFOAs are acquainted. Instead, *follow your curiosity*. And let's add joy here, too.

Why curiosity and joy? Because, as we've learned, curiosity and joy are the best proxies we have for (True, Directional) purpose. Curiosity and joy are the building blocks of fulfillment. They are the language of the True Self, and we very much want our True Selves leading the way on the Something Bigger front.

I asked Lyla to take out her notebook.

The Big Direction Process

It's hard to know where to begin when forming your Big Direction hypothesis, so what I'll be sharing with you in the pages that follow is a Big Direction–finding process. It's designed to help you recognize where your curiosity is leading you at the macro level and what your True Self is saying about your Something Bigger. It will also help you bypass your Fear Self, so you can actually hear what your True Self is saying.

You'll be walking through this process alongside my client Lyla, so it will be as if you're in the room with me going through this work step-by-step. For each exercise, you'll see the instructions—for Lyla and for you—then Lyla's responses, followed by space for yours, where appropriate.

Many of the upcoming prompts have been inspired and informed by others' work. I'm not the first person in the history of the world to ask these questions, of course. But I've selected what I've found to be the most effective and powerful inquiries and exercises and modified them specifically for UFOAs.

There are two parts to this process: the investigation and the analysis. Treat the first part like a brainstorm. Try things on. We want you to bring that "first draft" energy of breakthrough and possibility. This is a thought exercise about where your curiosity lies, *not* about what is practical or realistic. Or even where you may ultimately want to take action. No one is asking you to commit to anything that you come up with here; this is a commitment-free zone.

What's crucial is that your Fear Self isn't invited to this part of the process. Do your best to check all your "shoulds" at the door. All fears and feelings are valid; they're also not useful in the thought-experiment phase. There's nothing "unsafe" about just imagining doing something, which is what we're doing here, but your Fear Self isn't sophisticated enough to make that distinction. It will likely get agitated, telling you all the reasons why you can't and shouldn't and won't. Whatever your specific Fear Self go-to is—whether it's calling you naive, or dumb, or frivolous, or entitled, or selfish—it's very likely to show up during this exercise. Fear Self's gonna fear.

Remember, your Fear Self will resist *all* change; it doesn't matter what that is. Your Fear Self is not a reliable narrator about what is and isn't right for you. Rest assured that you can come back and re-evaluate every single hesitation and pressure-test to your heart's content anything you decide to actually move toward later. Before you begin, this would be a great time to apply some of the fear-slaying techniques you'll find at the end of this book, on page 261, to help yourself get in the most Trued mindset possible.

After you've completed the entire investigation process, the next part is the review. It requires some sleuthing and detective work, and personally, it is the part that I find to be the most fun. Instead of looking for your "purpose," you'll look for your "purpose patterns," or a few possible Big Directions you could go in.

What you're looking for when it comes to your Big Direction, and every step of this process, is that warmer feeling—something that lights you up, that feels light and right, that screams "Hell yes!" Your Big Direction is the thing that feels energizing and makes you want to get on the road, the thing that you can't *not* do.

It's possible that—for right now, at least—this feeling is completely inaccessible and only aspirational. Don't worry. If you've never let yourself feel this before, as so many of us haven't, or if you've previously seen those feelings as signs that something is a frivolous endeavor, then this may be way too big of a leap for today. That's okay. If you're very far from your True Something Bigger, as I was, it might just be the thing that you're a little bit more interested in and excited about than anything else. Look for the thought or the idea that piques your curiosity by any amount, even by only 1 percent. Initially, I wasn't bowled over with joy when the idea of taking a coaching training class occurred to me. I was, however, more curious about it than anything else I'd come across, and the idea simply wouldn't stop (annoyingly) popping into my thoughts. That was enough.

Lastly, remember the Principle of the First Draft. It's not about getting your Big Direction exactly right (there's no such thing), it's about forming a Directionally right life hypothesis. A best guess. A warmer theory. Write down everything that comes up for you, and do the sorting later. Do attempt to respond to every prompt in earnest, but know, too, that not every question is going to resonate with every person. If one really doesn't land, skip it, and come back later (or don't). It's not going to make or break the effectiveness of the exercise. Try not to let yourself get bogged down in getting it perfect or wondering if you're doing it right—that's likely your Fear Self stalling. If you find yourself getting stuck, come back to your curiosity and the prompt at hand, and keep going. And please don't make the relatively arbitrary amount of space offered an upper or lower limit for your own work. If you run out of space, just continue in a digital or analog notebook.

Don't fret if your responses feel repetitive; you don't have to come up with brand-new ideas for each question. These prompts are designed to get at the same things from different angles, so some repetition makes sense. Write it all down anyway. On the flip side, don't stress if nothing seems connected. Just write. We'll sort it out later.

Let's go!

PART ONE: THE HOT SPOTS

The first part is a series of five rapid-fire brainstorming prompts designed to get at your True Self "hot spots"—your most aligned, Directionally right moments and topics—from a variety of different angles. It's sort of like a True Self highlight reel. The key here is not to take them too seriously and not to limit yourself by what is "practical" or "possible." Remember, no one is asking you to actually commit to doing any of the things listed here. This is simply a generative thought exercise. We are only unearthing "clues." It doesn't need to "make sense" or "add up" quite yet. Have fun with this!

1. **Full Aliveness:** When was the last instance (or couple of instances) you felt fully alive—firing on all cylinders, losing track of time, forgetting-to-go-to-the-bathroom-or-check-your-phone kind of alive? Can you think of an instance when you were so sure that something was exactly what you were meant to be doing and where you were supposed to be? What was it like? (This could be professional or personal—giving a presentation, analyzing data in a spreadsheet, mentoring a younger colleague, dinner with a friend, walking down the street by yourself, dancing at a Beyoncé concert, sitting in your bathtub, eating a cookie . . . whatever!) List as many as you can think of, but shoot for at least five, in just a few minutes.

Lyla's Full Aliveness

- My recent community-building consulting project with a Jewish org—the most engaged I've been at work in a long time.

- Coffee date with my former assistant—mentoring/sponsoring younger women.

- Officiating my best friend's wedding.

- Recent meditation retreat.

- My monthly How Are You Doing, Really? group, a women's group that I started a few years ago and the highlight of my month every month. (The vulnerability and the honesty and the connection and the support of this group are unmatched anywhere else in my life.)

- Last blog post I wrote about what "community" really is and why it matters to me in the larger sense.

Your Full Aliveness

_____
_____
_____
_____
_____
_____
_____
_____
_____
_____

2. **Browsing History:** What "random" types of content do you find yourself getting lost in? Not what you "have to" read or listen to professionally but the type of stuff that you escape into or browse "just for you." If I looked at what tabs you have open or the types of articles that you're usually saving for later, what might I find? What types of podcasts do you subscribe to? If I looked at your "Recommended for You" podcasts, what would I notice? Where and when do you go down

Instagram (or TikTok or X or Threads) rabbit holes? What types of accounts? Any specific accounts? If I scrolled through what you're following on the social media platform of your choice, what themes might I find? (And I'm not talking about "hate following.") What are your favorite newsletters that you almost always actually open? See if you notice content themes that feel "warmer" or "light and right" and that leave you wholly inspired or fully spark your curiosity!

Lyla's Browsing History

- All the kinds of stuff you might see on Oprah's *Super Soul Sunday* (sorry, not sorry).

- Instagram therapists and personal growth stuff.

- Lit mag Instagram accounts, like @ParisReview.

- Medicinal herbalist accounts.

- Midwife and doula education accounts.

- Therapy and spirituality podcasts: *On Being with Krista Tippett*; *Where Should We Begin?* with Esther Perel; *Unlocking Us* and *Dare to Lead* with Brené Brown; and *We Can Do Hard Things* with Glennon Doyle.

- Podcasts on Judaism: *Jewitches, Chutzpod!, Unholy,* and *Judaism Unbound.*

- Current tabs: a guided-meditation video from Tara Brach, a recent poem in *The New Yorker*, a how-to article on starting your own medicinal herb garden.

- Newsletters: *Daily Stoic*, Rabbi Danya Ruttenberg's *Life is a Sacred Text*, *The Marginalian* by Maria Popova, Priya Parker's *Art of Gathering*, Anne Helen Petersen's *Culture Study.*

Your Browsing History

_____

_____

_____

_____

_____

_____

_____

_____

_____

3. **If I Could Get Paid for This:** Is there a topic, hobby, habit, or activity that made you think, *I wish I could get paid to do this?* Something that you do so naturally and regularly, or just enjoy so much, that it would be one of those elusive you'll-never-work-a-day-in-your-life things? Whether this thought has occurred to you in the past, see if you can think of a few of these things now. Totally unpractical, as always, is great! You don't need to be able to think of a way to monetize it. (PSA: Your argumentative Fear Self will probably pop in to say, "But that will ruin it for you! It won't be fun anymore if it becomes your 'job'!" Maybe, maybe not. Either way, it doesn't matter here because we are just brainstorming, not actually trying to turn any of these things into your job. It's just about the investigation and the clues.)

Examples: eating out at restaurants → food critic, looking at art → private curator, traveling → travel writer, playing pickleball → sponsored professional pickleball player, doomscrolling → culture critic

Lyla's "If I Could Get Paid for This" List

- Talk to people about their stuff → be a therapist.

- Puzzle through life's big questions with other women → group therapist; coach; facilitate my own discussion groups.

- Herbal medicine → grow an herb garden and make medicinal herbal tinctures.

- Read/listen/study and research spirituality and philosophy and personal growth → become some kind of researcher or professor or author; go back to school for one of these things.

- Make restaurant recommendations for specific scenarios → build a restaurant recommendation engine or some sort of concierge or travel consultant.

- Build communities → find a new way to do community-building.

Your "If I Could Get Paid for This" List

4. **Back to School:** If you *had* to go back a to school or learn something new, what would it be? It doesn't have to be a traditional advanced degree, if that doesn't appeal. It could be a certification, or online learning, or a trade, or a skill, or an apprenticeship, or a single class. Assume you have all the money and time you need for this, and there is no obligation to "do" anything with what you learn, especially in terms of a career.

Lyla's Back to School List

- Divinity school
- Master's in social work or psychology
- Herbal medicine training
- Midwifery training
- Voice lessons

Your Back to School List

5. **Little You:** What did you love to do at age eight (or six or ten or twelve)? What were you best at? What did people notice about you at that age? What is the family lore about you growing up? What would little you find most surprising about your life today? What would that younger self be most disappointed by? Delighted by? Fully approving of?

Lyla's Little You

- Constantly asking about the meaning of life and why we are here and what happens after we die.

- Loved forming "clubs" à la the Baby-Sitters Club and being president, obviously.

- Constantly thinking about ways to make money and things to sell—lemonade stands, jewelry making, tie-dyeing clothes, wildflower bouquets, a soda-can return business . . .

- Loved knowing people's secrets and being the person to whom they told secrets.

- Loved Hebrew school.

- Loved singing.

- Little me would be disappointed that I'm unhappy and stuck.

- She'd be delighted that my work is about "big girl clubs."

Your Little You

_____

_____

_____

_____

_____

_____

_____

_____

_____

_____

PART TWO: JEALOUSY JUICING

Jealousy is an emotion from which we tend to run away and label as "bad." However, like all emotions, jealousy holds important information for us. For this exercise, jealousy just means "I want what you have in my own life." If we are coming at it not from a place of scarcity but from a place of possibility—which, of course, in a Directional world, we are—it's not a zero-sum game. Our wanting something takes nothing away from the other person who has it, and the fact that someone else found something we want is fabulous news—this means that it exists and is possible, and if they can have it, there's no reason we can't, too!

This exercise is one that the great Julia Cameron uses in _The Artist's Way_ as well. Today, instead of avoiding your jealousy, you want to scavenge for as much "jealousy" as you possibly can. On a separate page or spreadsheet, create three columns and ask yourself the following questions:

> Column 1: _Who makes me jealous?_ Create a list of all the people you hold jealousy toward or those who have what you want. Shoot for ten to start.

Example: Sarah, a wealthy and successful photographer.

Column 2: *Why am I jealous of this person?*

Example: She has a thriving career as a photographer.

Column 3: *What is one thing I can do to have more of that thing?* It doesn't matter if you know how to do that thing or whether you think you can actually do more of it.

Example: Take steps toward getting paid for some photos; maybe list on Etsy.

Lyla's Jealousy Juicing

Person	Why/What I Want More Of	Possible Actions
My therapist friend	She's so fulfilled by her work and never questions her value; she truly changes people's lives in meaningful ways; she helps real humans, not businesses.	-Mentor more people -Work with individuals -Become a therapist -Do fulfilling work
My rabbi	She gets to think and talk about interesting spiritual stuff all day with groups and individuals; she is involved with the most important and sacred moments and rites of passage in people's lives; she provides spiritual guidance to people.	-Get more involved in some Jewish communities -Become a rabbi -Do more individual mentorship and facilitate more groups of some kind

Krista Tippett	She also gets to think about interesting spiritual and philosophical stuff all day; she interviews incredible people from all walks of life; she is always learning and exploring and making new connections; she helps people on a large scale.	-Explore doing some sort of content creation (a podcast or a blog, maybe) -Interview interesting people about interesting stuff
My friend	She's an interior designer with the absolute best taste, and every time I go to her apartment, I just think about how good it would feel to live there.	-Get an interior designer -Ask Sue for help decorating
My friends who have nieces and nephews	I don't want to have children myself, but I would love to be close to some children and have a lifelong relationship with them; my friends who have nieces and nephews all do that (have them come stay for a week in the summer or for their birthdays, go to all the dance recitals and school plays and graduations, etc.); I want to be a trusted adult in some young people's lives.	-Harass my sister about having children (LOL) -Reach out to a few close friends and express that I'd love to support them and their kids in a more consistent and meaningful way

| Adele | She has the most incredible voice and gets to sing for a living. | -Join some sort of singing group
-Take voice lessons
-Record something just for fun |

PART THREE: SLIDING DOORS

If you weren't doing what you're doing now, what else would you be doing? In a parallel universe, what might your alternative career and/or life be? Or who might you choose to "come back" as? Another way of asking this question is: If your job, your company, and your entire industry were suddenly wiped out of existence (use your imagination for the narrative here—maybe AI took over, or there was a pandemic), what would you think about doing next? List ten things.

Reminder: Don't think too long and hard. In fact, set a timer for five minutes. Like the other exercises, this is not meant to be something that you then directly translate to going out and doing in real life. Put that Fear Self away. The key word here is *imaginary*. We are exploring, not making a ten-year plan!

Examples: fashion designer, florist, photographer, field worker for the Clinton Global Initiative, acupuncturist, restaurateur, epidemiologist, Freddie Mercury, food critic, preschool teacher, Terry Gross, graphic designer, senator, Gloria Steinem, documentary filmmaker, professor of pop culture

Lyla's Sliding Doors

1. Spirituality/philosophy podcast host like Krista Tippett with *On Being*

2. Psychologist

3. Divinity school

4. Poet

5. Nonfiction author

6. Midwife

7. Psychic/medium (I would love to be able to talk to the other side!)

8. Medicinal herbalist

9. Lighthouse keeper who lives in a lighthouse (I have no idea why; I've just always wanted to do this!)

10. Adele

Your Sliding Doors

1. _____
2. _____
3. _____
4. _____
5. _____
6. _____
7. _____
8. _____
9. _____
10. _____

PART FOUR: THE SPONSORED LIFE

Imagine that I have a wonderful surprise for you: you have an anonymous patron, a sponsor who sees your value and your worth and invests in you and your life. No strings attached and no pressure to "produce." Time and money are now no object. You can invest your resources on absolutely anything. How might you spend your time? Where would you start in the first six months? What might you explore? If you don't know, what steps might you take to figure it out?

If you're inclined to answer "Do nothing" or "Retire early," great! I'm all about that. But, also, you have to spend your time . . . somehow. In this case, what "leisure" activities would you do? Get specific. If the answer is to take hammock naps, drink mai tais, hang out with friends and family, read graphic novels, and watch sunsets, write that!

Then, try asking yourself *And then what?* a few times, and see what comes up.

When most UFOAs complete this exercise, it becomes clear that the longing for Something Bigger doesn't go away when the necessity of income does. In six to twelve months, even the most burned-out UFOAs tend to get bored, and once more, they find themselves craving contribution and impact and meaning. But the remedy can be as simple as planting a garden, fostering animals, running for local office, learning to play the piano, renovating a house, or caring for grandchildren. And it can also be something more externally facing, like making a documentary, starting a foundation, or traveling around the world to spread specialized knowledge as the world's foremost expert on the entomology of bees.

Lyla's Sponsored Life

1. Take a sabbatical from my business and leave it in the hands of my right-hand person, to whom I've taught everything I know.

2. Start two or three more How Are You Doing, Really? groups with different women, so I'd be going to one a week.

3. Write every day to see what comes out and what, if any, stories I want to tell.

4. Go to school for all the things I listed in part one (master's in social work, divinity degree, midwife degree, herbal medicine training).

5. Plant a medicinal herb garden.

6. Write and record an album.

7. Attend a childbirth.

8. Shadow my rabbi.

9. Go on an extended meditation retreat.

10. Go to surf camp and learn to surf.

Your Sponsored Life

_____

_____

_____

_____

_____

_____

_____

_____

PART FIVE: FRIENDS AND FAMILY FEEDBACK

In this exercise, you get to take a break and make your friends and family do some work on your behalf! In truth, this can be one of the most meaningful, not to mention useful, exercises in the entire process. My clients routinely tell me that this experience ranks up there with the ones they remember—and value—most.

The people around us have the most unadulterated knowledge base for us about how and where we are most impactful in the world. This is another great way to bypass our Fear Self because, well, our Fear Self can't exist outside us, obviously. It is so rare that we have the opportunity to ask the people who love us for their feedback or to help us acknowledge the things we do well organically. This is your opportunity to crowdsource in an aligned way! I promise that this will throw you some surprises, so get ready. Of course, this is still subjective, so it doesn't mean that they are "right" about everything, but it is useful information to consider in this stage of the process.

Think of five to ten people who know you well, from different stages of your life. Try to pick people who you feel are likely to see you clearly and have the most insight, even if they are not actually those who know you the most intimately (though they can be, too).

Send them an email or a text (or give them a call or visit them in person—whatever you feel comfortable with) to ask:

- *What do you think I do best or most naturally?*
- *What would you say is (are) my "superpower(s)"?*

- *When, or for what, do you think of me first? Nothing is too big or too small. If you have examples that stick out in your mind, those would be a big help, too!*

Assure them that this doesn't have to be all-encompassing or overthought, and it doesn't have to be restricted to "professional" skills. Your superpower can be making the most perfect quiche, being an expert baby swaddler, or picking out the best gifts. "Strong leader," "great communicator," and "great people manager" are excellent, too. For context, you may want to explain that you are doing an exercise from a book—use me as an excuse!

Lyla's Feedback List

- "Rare combination of vision and execution in business."

- "Community builder, obvi! You're an incredibly gifted networker (and I mean that in the most organic and genuine sense of the word), and you seem to know everyone and are great at connecting the right people. I usually say no to random intros people want to make, but I will always, always say yes to yours because they are always the most fruitful and incredible connections."

- "Incredible soul friend—everyone should get to have a friend like you—nonjudgmental witness when I need that, sees me so clearly and reflects that back to me when I need that, not afraid of even my hardest and most painful emotions, great life problem-solver, seems to know what I need before I do, vulnerable and open and reciprocal, not afraid of having hard convos when stuff comes up. Just an all-around great platonic life partner!"

- "The most fun person to ponder life with—whenever I need a good zoom out and some perspective, or am dealing with Big Feelings or Big Questions, you're the person I call."

- "Makes the best chocolate chip cookies!"

- "Best-kept secret: you have an amazing singing voice!"

- "The most supportive mentor and manager I've ever had."

- "Walks the walk—so much integrity."

- "The monthly How Are You Doing, Really? women's group you created is the most transformative and life-changing thing that has ever happened to me, and I'll never be able to thank you enough for what you've created in our little group."

- "You changed the way I thought about women and female friendship. Before you, I thought I was a 'guy's girl' and didn't trust women, and you changed all of that. I have so many flourishing female friendships now that are the most important things in my life."

- "Reliable and consistent and trustworthy."

- "I can't believe how many of the most creative ideas come from your brain."

- "The most brilliant community and social mind I've ever seen."

- "Leadership, entrepreneurship, connection."

- "A great teacher!"

- "I would love to see you leading your own community!"

I'd suggest collecting all of your feedback in a doc or a folder somewhere so you can save the responses in full, but for now, jot down here a couple of the key words, or phrases, once you've received them.

Your Feedback List

_____

_____

_____

_____

_____

_____

_____

_____

_____

_____

_____

INVESTIGATING PURPOSE PATTERNS

Now, it's purpose-pattern investigation time. Lyla and I sat down with some highlighters and went through all her responses together, searching for her purpose patterns and clues to her potential next Big Direction hypothesis. We would list each thematic pattern we uncovered, as well as noting exactly where it came up.

First, we highlighted the themes that were already playing a significant role in Lyla's life. It's not that we wanted to rule these out. Rather, we knew that they weren't her Something Bigger, at least not on their own.

Lyla's Purpose Patterns v1

1. Community Building

2. Entrepreneurship/Business

Next, we noted the few clear and straightforward themes that jumped out right away.

> 3. Health and Wellness: Herbal Medicine and Midwifery (Particularly Women's Health)
>
> • *Browsing History, Back to School, Sliding Doors,* and *The Sponsored Life*
>
> 4. Writing
>
> • *Full Aliveness:* Recent blog post about what "community" really is and why it matters to me in the larger sense
>
> • *If I Could Get Paid for This:* Study and research spirituality and philosophy
>
> • *Sliding Doors:* Poet, nonfiction author
>
> • *The Sponsored Life:* Write every day to see what comes out and what, if any, stories I want to tell
>
> 5. Singing
>
> • *Back to School:* Voice lessons
>
> • *Jealousy Juicing:* Adele
>
> • *The Sponsored Life:* Record an album
>
> • *Friends and Family Feedback:*
>
>> • "Best-kept secret: you have an amazing singing voice!"

Finally, we looked at what was left and sifted through these until a new hypothesis started to emerge.

Not every item needs to fit into a pattern. Surf lessons didn't make it, for example, and neither did chocolate chip cookies. They could have—it's possible that they each needed to become their own theme or that these joy sparkers contained information that was relevant to what Lyla needs more of in her life, like the orderliness and "rules" of baking or the "ride the wave" philosophy and going-with-the-flowness of surfing. But they weren't feeling as "warm" and as compelling to Lyla as some of the other patterns.

6. Individual Counseling/Mentorship/Therapy

- *Full Aliveness:* Mentoring/sponsoring former assistant

- *Browsing History:* Instagram therapists and personal-growth accounts and pods

- *If I Could Get Paid for This:* Talk to people about their stuff/be a therapist

- *Back to School:* Get a master's in social work

- *Little You:* Loved knowing people's secrets and being the person they told secrets to

- *Jealousy Juicing:* Therapist, rabbi

- *Sliding Doors:* Psychologist

- *The Sponsored Life:* Get a master's in social work

- *Friends and Family Feedback:*

  - "Incredible soul friend—everyone should get to have a friend like you—nonjudgmental witness when I need that, sees me so clearly and reflects that back to me when I need that, not afraid of even my hardest and most painful emotions, great life problem-solver, seems to know what I need before I do, vulnerable and open and reciprocal, not afraid of having hard convos when stuff comes up. Just an all-around great platonic life partner!"

- "The most fun person to ponder life with— whenever I need a good zoom out and some perspective, or am dealing with Big Feelings or Big Questions, you're the person I call."

- "The most supportive mentor and manager I've ever had."

The next one, Spirituality/Philosophy, was everywhere. It showed up in some obvious ways: Lyla's interest in divinity school, her browsing interests, her desire to get paid to read about and research spirituality and philosophy or "puzzle through life's big questions." But it also surfaced in some more subtle hot spots: the enjoyment of her consulting work for a Jewish organization, the officiation of her best friend's wedding, and her younger self's intense curiosity about the meaning of life. Meditation retreats also came up several times.

7. **Spirituality/Philosophy** (meaning of life, Big Qs, the sacred/ceremony/rites of passage)

- *Full Aliveness:* Consulting project with a Jewish org, officiating my best friend's wedding, recent meditation retreat

- *Browsing History:* Therapy and spirituality podcasts; podcasts on Judaism; a guided-meditation video from Tara Brach in my current tabs; philosophy newsletters

- *If I Could Get Paid for This:* Puzzle through life's big questions with other women; read/listen/study and research about spirituality and philosophy and personal growth

- *Back to School:* Divinity school

- *Little You:* Constantly asking about the meaning of life and why we are here and what happens after we die; loved Hebrew school

- *Jealousy Juicing:* My rabbi; Krista Tippett (spirituality and philosophy podcast host with a master's in divinity)

- *Sliding Doors:* Spirituality/philosophy podcast host like Krista Tippett with *On Being*, divinity school, psychic/medium

- *The Sponsored Life:* Go to divinity school, shadow my rabbi, go on an extended meditation retreat

- *Friends and Family Feedback:*

  - "The most fun person to ponder life with—whenever I need a good zoom out and some perspective, or am dealing with Big Feelings or Big Questions, you're the person I call."

  - "Walks the walk—so much integrity."

The eighth one was Judaism and it could potentially be a subset of the previous category of spirituality, like "Jewish spirituality," or it could be its own Big Direction, like "Jewish cultural organizations." For now, we decided it was worth separating out as its own possible purpose pattern.

8. Judaism

- *Full Aliveness:* Consulting project with a Jewish org

• *Browsing History:* Podcasts on Judaism, Rabbi Danya Ruttenberg's *Life is a Sacred Text*

• *Little You:* Loved Hebrew school

• *Jealousy Juicing:* My rabbi

• *The Sponsored Life:* Shadow my rabbi

9. Leader of a Community/Facilitator of Groups/ Connection + Vulnerability

• *Full Aliveness:* My monthly How Are You Doing, Really? women's group

• *If I Could Get Paid for This:* Puzzle through life's big questions with other women

• *Little You:* Loved forming "clubs"

• *Jealousy Juicing:* [My rabbi] gets to think and talk about interesting spiritual shit all day with groups and individuals

• *The Sponsored Life:* Start two or three more How Are You Doing, Really? groups with different women, so I'd be going to one a week

• *Friends and Family Feedback:*

  • "The monthly How Are You Doing, Really? women's group you created is the most transformative and life-changing thing that has ever happened to me, and I'll never be able to thank you enough for what you've created in little group."

  • "You changed the way I thought about women and female friendship. Before you, I thought I was a 'guy's girl' and didn't trust women, and you changed all of that. I have so many flourishing female friendships now that are the most important things in my life."

- "The most brilliant community and social mind I've ever seen."

- "Leadership, entrepreneurship, connection."

- "A great teacher!"

- "I would love to see you leading your own community!"

As we got further into identifying these patterns, Lyla's energy grew. The deeper into the analysis we got, the warmer we got. As she read that last comment from her Friends and Family Feedback exercise—"I would love to see you leading your own community!"—something clicked for her. We began to wonder together if, instead of building other people's communities, her Big Direction was rather to focus on building her own community. Not so much a departure as an evolution.

With Lyla, we just needed to update the Big Direction file. She had been heading toward her Something Bigger, but she had stopped updating it! She forgot that it was Directional and not Destinational. She stopped letting it evolve. It was as if she'd unplugged her Inner Navigation System once she'd arrived at what she was told was "success." She turned her once Directionally right, aligned ambition into a destination and permanently inhabited somewhere that was supposed to be but a stop along the way. Sometimes, it's turning the Inner Navigation System on for the first time. Other times, it's just finding the signal again. The process works regardless.

In Lyla's case, we had a lot of possible directions. Usually, it's between one and four. More directions, by the way, is not necessarily better—it only takes one! You're not doing anything wrong if you don't have more than a few Big Direction hypotheses. You'll recall that AOC had three or four, and only one that really turned out to be compelling at that moment in time.

We assembled the complete list of purpose patterns in preparation for the last step of this process: determining which Big Direction(s) to move toward.

Lyla's Purpose Patterns v1

1. Community Building

2. Entrepreneurship/Business

3. Health and Wellness: Herbal Medicine and Midwifery (Particularly Women's Health)

4. Writing

5. Singing

6. Individual Counseling/Mentorship/Therapy

7. Spirituality/Philosophy

8. Judaism

9. Leader of a Community/Facilitator of Groups/Connection + Vulnerability

To narrow it down, we use our trusty Align process from phase two to "try on" each of the possible Big Directions to see which one(s) feel the warmest. We're looking for those that feel the most exciting and hold the most curiosity as *hypotheses*, not as commitments.

Another way of asking this is: Which of these would stir up dis-appointment if you did *not* look into them further? Or, if you're someone who has a lot of patterns, like Lyla, which of these do you want to explore *first*, knowing that this list isn't going anywhere and that you can come back to any and all possibilities that you're still curious about later?

Also keep in mind that, even if we can't see it now, several of these Big Directions may converge. When I see a list like this, I im-mediately start seeing potential combinations, like Lyla not only leading a counseling community centered around Jewish spirituality but also writing and singing about these themes as a part of this work. Or maybe she incorporates herbal medicine and midwifery practices, as well as individual counseling and group work, into the services of a community center dedicated to women's mental and physical health. I ended up combining several of my patterns (coun-seling/advising/therapy, writing, business/entrepreneurship) into cre-ating a coaching methodology, building a business around it, and writing about it. There are infinite permutations of this, and the goal isn't to "figure it out" or to try to formulate a hypothesis that maxi-mizes the number of pathways we can include. This notion is meant to be liberating—you don't need to choose one path at the expense of all others. Our job right now is only to "go where it's warm" and to pick the direction(s) that we feel the most energy around and the strongest pull toward exploring.

I had Lyla try on each one and report back from her INS. It was clear that the warmest, most aligned, light-and-right, I'd-be-so-sad-if-I-didn't-explore-this vibes were emanating from the last three or four. (She chose to combine Judaism with spirituality for now, as that felt right to her.)

Lyla's Purpose Patterns v2

• Individual Counseling/Mentorship/Therapy

• Spirituality/Philosophy (including Judaism)

• Leader of a Community/Facilitator of Groups

Lyla lit up when imagining all the possibilities ahead and eagerly started brainstorming where she might begin. Her entire demeanor—her energy, her affect, her body language, the way she spoke, her level of engagement—were dramatically different from those of the woman who had first walked in mourning her lost purpose. That's how you know you're back in alignment, heading toward your Something Bigger.

You've likely noticed that this is not a definitive job title, or even a solid plan. It's not "Vancouver," and it's certainly not as specific as 123 Grand Street. It's just the Big Direction: north. Your life hypothesis will be something like "Dogs" or maybe eventually "Dog Training" or "Dog Grooming," but it likely won't be "Head Judge of the Terrier Group at the National Dog Show." We want your Big Direction to be wide and spacious with plenty of room for movement. It's not particularly actionable (yet), and that's by design. Actionability is what happens next. Now, armed with a couple of Directional Life hypotheses, we can get into action and start driving in the dark.

Your Turn: Identifying Your Purpose Patterns

You've done the majority of the work for your Big Direction already. Phew! Take a break. Put it aside. Do one of the fear-slaying exercises from page 261 if that feels good.

When you're ready—whether that's in five minutes, a day, or a week—go back and review each of these five Big Direction–seeking steps that you've completed and look for any patterns, repeating themes, or trends. You may find it helpful to use different-colored highlighters or pens, one for each theme. Refer to Lyla's process for inspiration and guidance.

If you're feeling stuck or not seeing any patterns, let it marinate for a bit, and come back with fresh eyes on another day. I promise that the patterns will emerge—don't force it!

You may also find it helpful to bring a trusted friend to search with you. Sometimes, we're too close to it, but the patterns are obvious to someone who is not us.

Keep in mind that your answers don't have to be literal. Get sleuthy. For example, Mark Manson, the author of *The Subtle Art of Not Giving a F*ck*, talks about how when he first started thinking about what he might do as a profession, the only thing that he knew he loved to do was play video games. To use my language, video games were a big "hot spot" for him. However, that did not necessarily mean he was supposed to become a full-time gamer, which didn't feel warmer for him. It could have, but it didn't. If he had limited himself to considering "clues" that were direct translations, he wouldn't have considered the lessons he had gathered from gaming. What he saw in his love for gaming was a drive for improvement, progress, and competition. Self-improvement and personal progress, applied more broadly, became his Big Direction, and he started researching and talking about *that* topic, eventually publishing many books. Another person may have also had video games as a hot spot, but maybe it was the fantasy worlds that really engaged them. Still another may have discovered that it was about the graphic design. The same clue can lead different people toward very different potential Big Directions to explore.

If nothing is appearing on the surface level, play with going a level deeper by asking: *What about this feels warmer? What specific parts of this pique my curiosity or elicit joy?*

By reviewing your answers from the Big Direction process, identify some possible purpose patterns that you're noticing and list them here:

1. _____
2. _____
3. _____
4. _____
5. _____

Phase V: Iterate

Taking Aligned Action

Here's where the real experimenting begins.

You've learned how to think Directionally. Now you'll begin to move through your life Directionally by taking *aligned action*. In this culminating phase of UFOA recovery and Directional Living school, we're iterating on the Big Direction hypotheses you've uncovered in the last phase.

This perma-phase, which is where you'll ideally be living most of the time from here on out, is all about testing and learning, launching and iterating. It builds on everything you've done so far. Now you'll start taking aligned action (Iterate) toward your Something Bigger direction (Orient) based on the guidance of your calibrated and trued Inner Navigation System (Align), having cleared the way of any *mis*alignments (Release).

Directional Living is about to come to life, tangibly and visibly. You'll begin to see all the internal work you've been doing taking shape in your external life. It's here where we shift from brainstorming and the hypothetical to experiencing tangible transformation. This is where we *make it real.*

This phase comes as a relief to most action-oriented, get-shit-done overachiever types who have been champing at the bit to execute already. Forward motion there will be! But this is likely going to feel different from any other "action plan" you've made before.

How do we translate our Big Direction off in the distance into this phase's single next Directionally right, aligned action? Put aside everything you think you know about what it means to "make it happen" in your life. Typically, the energy of UFOA Destinational action, of "getting it done," is willpower, brute force, effort, manipulation, and just constantly trying really freaking hard. Living Directionally, on the other hand, is about engaging in an ongoing conversation with your life. You are co-creating the unfolding of your life in real time, in partnership with the world around you. Like any true dialogue, it's collaborative and dynamic; there is a feedback loop.

The real art of Directional Living, just like the art of conversation, is in the co-creation: it's about paying full attention without an agenda, being present with and responding to what is, not just waiting for your turn to talk. You may think you know the topic of this conversation (your Big Direction), and you may even have a sense of how the discussion will go, but you don't get to dictate the conversation according to how you alone would like things to transpire. The true magic of a co-creative conversation, whether between two people or between you and your life, is that it leads to a level of new understanding that is inevitably more beautiful, inspiring, and expansive than you could have ever imagined on your own.

You can think of the Directional co-creative process like playing tennis with the universe, but a just-for-fun scoreless rally in which the goal is simply to keep the ball in play. You can't necessarily predict where and how and when the ball will come back to you. You certainly can't run to the other side of the net in an attempt to control the returning shot. And you can't play both sides of the net, no matter how hard you try or want to. What a relief it can be to realize that you're only responsible for your own side of the net!

We UFOAs tend to not even realize that we're trying to control the entire game, because through one of its greatest tricks, Destinational Living convinced us that we're playing a solo game, just hitting a ball against a wall. Directional Living, on the other hand, helps us see that life isn't a game that can be played alone. Our lives don't exist in a vacuum outside the context of the world in which we live. Co-creation—being in dynamic and collaborative Directional process—is what allows us to be responsive to the (always) changing environment, both inside and outside us, in real time, instead of insisting that it must be static and fixed. It's what puts us in an active and alive relationship with what is actually happening in the world and within ourselves. Co-creation is the opposite of control.

There's a genuine humility and patience required for this approach, an admission of and tolerance for the feeling of not knowing *yet*. I love the beautiful and simple name for this in Zen Buddhism: "don't-know mind." The energy of taking Directional action is not forcing or controlling, but rather allowing, giving the necessary time and space for a process to unfold *without manipulation*. "Without manipulation" is the operative phrase here, and this is typically very hard for us UFOAs. In Directional Living, our job is to *allow* the Directional path, not to force the Destinational one. Here, you are making a conscious and intentional choice to stay on your side of the net and allow whatever is returned to you.

The Lily Pad Approach

In Directional Living, we hold two things, and only two things, in mind at once: the Big Direction hypothesis pointing us into the distance, and the single next aligned action immediately in front of us. Whatever happens in between those two things is not our concern.

Imagine that you're playing *Directional Living: The Video Game*. In said game, your little avatar is standing on the bank of a huge river with the objective of getting to the other side. You may not know exactly what's on the other side, or exactly where you'll land, specifically, but you know that in order to progress, you must traverse this river. You notice a lily pad that you can easily reach, but you have no idea where you'd go from this one solitary lily pad, so you have your little avatar running up and down the river bank trying everything you can think of to help you get across with certainty but to no avail.

Eventually, exasperated, you take a step out onto this single, visible lily pad. To your surprise, not only does the lily pad hold your weight, but as soon as you're on it, a second lily pad appears. When you reach the second lily pad, the third appears, and so on and so forth. The trick is that you only get to see one lily pad at a time. There isn't a perfectly plotted lily pad path across the river that you can scope out in entirety before you begin. You must take a step and *allow* the next lily pad to emerge. It requires us to trust that there is, in fact, a lily pad path across the river. We must embody don't-know mind. The key is to remember that the higher intelligence of the game knows the winning path across the lake, even if we don't.

I call this the Lily Pad Approach. Take a step and let go of the results. Or as Rumi said (and yes, I'm that person quoting Rumi in a self-helpish book): "As you start to walk on the way, the way appears." Why does this work? The more you true yourself and listen for and to your INS, the more quickly you're able to recognize and trust what is alignment for you. Alignment begets more alignment, while misalignment begets more misalignment. Warmer actions beget more warmer actions, and colder actions beget more colder actions. Directionally right actions beget Directionally right results. If you want to get at your aligned ambition, you need to take aligned actions. On the flip side of that, blind (Destinational) action can only beget blind ambition. The unlock here is that we really can focus on just the one lily pad in front of us, asking only, "Is this Directionally right?" Because Directionally right actions will *always* yield Directionally right results.

LYLA'S LILY PADS

To activate your Big Direction, you only need to initiate the first step. The first thing we want to do is identify that first lily pad, a single warmer, aligned action for one (or all) of your Big Direction hypotheses from the previous chapter.

Lyla and I revisited her possible Big Directions and began to brainstorm her first lily pads for each one.

Big Direction Hypothesis		First Lily Pad
1. Individual Counseling/ Mentorship/Therapy	→	_____
2. Spirituality/Philosophy (including Judaism)	→	_____
3. Leader of a Community/ Facilitator of Groups	→	_____

It's important not to get caught up in taking the "perfect" or the "correct" action here. Any Directionally right, warmer action—any amount warmer—will work brilliantly. If it's warmer—if it sparks curiosity or joy or eagerness—then you can't get it wrong. All we want to do right now is gather more information for our INS, which will cue a first lily pad and give us the momentum we need to keep going. The goal is simply to advance the plot. We're going for low-stakes, low-commitment actions here, such as researching psychology programs or talking to a therapist friend (not larger actions like putting down a deposit for a master's program, quitting a job, or moving to another country). This phase is called Iterate for a reason. We want to cultivate an experimental mindset in this phase, an incremental launch-and-iterate mentality.

Sometimes the hypothesis will easily lend itself to a first lily pad, and spotting that aligned action will feel obvious, as you'll see was the case for Lyla as soon as she started doing some basic internet research. If that's true for you, write it down on page 208 and take the step. Don't overcomplicate it! If it doesn't come quickly or easily, don't worry. We've got a formula for that, too.

For Lyla, the first two initial lily pads had to do with learning about graduate schools, both those with social work and psychology programs and those with divinity programs, to get a sense of what existed and what her options might be. The third lily pad from this initial batch was to start exploring a second community group based on the How Are You Doing, Really? one that she'd already started "just for fun." This meant outlining things about the group, like what its goals would be, how many people would participate, when and where it would meet, et cetera. Based on what she'd learned running the first group, how might this one differ? How might it be the same?

These were not Lyla's only initial lily pad possibilities. There were infinite first steps that she could have taken—people to reach out to, books to read, podcasts to listen to—but these were the ones about which Lyla was the most curious, the ones that felt "lightest and rightest" for her at that moment.

Big Direction Hypothesis		First Lily Pad
1. Individual Counseling/ Mentorship/Therapy	→	Research social work/ psych programs
2. Spirituality/Philosophy (including Judaism)	→	Research divinity schools
3. Leader of a Community/ Facilitator of Groups	→	Explore starting a second women's group

Your Turn: First Lily Pads

Big Direction Hypothesis (from last phase)		First Lily Pad
_____	→	_____
_____	→	_____
_____	→	_____
_____	→	_____
_____	→	_____

What we're looking for as you take each of these lily pad steps is both the facts *and* the feelings. You're not just on a fact-finding mission; pay attention, too, to how you feel internally as you try on each new possibility. The most important information that we get from each test-and-learn round in the Lily Pad Approach is not the tactical and logistical practicalities, such as application deadlines and program requirements, but instead the internal information generated by your INS's response to exposing yourself to new information. *How do I feel when I think about attending this school? How do I feel when I think about starting this group?* (The how-do-I-feel question is applicable to any context: *How do I feel about going on this date, adopting a vegan diet, traveling to that city, accepting that speaking opportunity, hiring that person, joining that club?*) Each lily pad offers your INS new data to translate into more accurate guidance toward the most aligned next step. You want to ask things like *Do I light up when I'm reading about one school but feel blah when reading about another?* and *Is one kind of program warmer and another colder?* This is the most valuable kind of information we can glean from a lily pad step, even if, and perhaps especially if, it's colder.

If Lyla starts to explore grad schools and finds herself bored and coming up with nothing of resonance, that's very important feedback! Don't ignore that information! That's a clear "colder," and that's going to result in a very different next iterative step than if she's staying up all night because she can't contain her excitement while looking through course catalogs.

Remember that you can only play your side of the court. This means releasing any expectations around the results and allowing the co-creative rally to unfold, without interference. Each aligned action is the equivalent of hitting the ball over the net. You've done your part. You don't get to—or need to!—determine what gets returned. It's impossible to play both sides of the court. Your job is to take aligned actions (Directional), *not* to manage outcomes (Destinational). The latter is overreach. This is what it means to be truly process-oriented—allowing the unfolding of the process—instead of being outcome-oriented, our old Four Omens foe.

In practice, this means that Lyla doesn't want to go into her exploration of graduate programs skewing the results to conform with what she thinks they *should* be. It's very common for someone in her position to want grad school to be The Thing, for example, so that she can be done with this whole soul-searching exercise, or for her to fixate on a specific grad school program that she thinks will be the easiest to explain to *others*. Taking the Lily Pad Approach is not declaring, "I should go to grad school, so let's find the most efficient path there," and then simply calculating the number of credit hours she would need to graduate. (Can you spot the UFOA-ness?!) Instead, it's about framing her investigation in the form of a far more qualitative, far more personal research question: *How does it feel— inside my body—to seriously consider going to grad school?*

Lyla also doesn't want to go into the vision brainstorm for her How Are You Doing, Really? community imagining what she thinks will scale the fastest or make the most money—that would be some big Destinational energy. The open-ended question she's exploring is not *Now that I've validated this business idea, how do I make it into something huge?* Instead, she's asking, *Is this a viable project that serves people meaningfully and also inspires me?* and *Am I curious about the unfolding of this?*

Pursuing the answers to these kinds of questions, Lyla discovered that divinity school (or something adjacent) felt the most Directionally right for her. Researching psychology and social work programs felt like drudgery. Yet when she looked into divinity schools, her curiosity sparked, and she was flooded with inspiration. The more she researched, the more research she wanted to do. It felt "light and right" and joyful to imagine this new possibility.

She also couldn't wait to tell me her thinking around her idea for the new How Are You Doing, Really? gatherings. What emerged was not a single group but a network of groups, a community. This was a natural extension of her community-building work, only here she would be creating and leading the community, not consulting on someone else's community, as one of her friends had suggested in the feedback exercise during the Orient phase. She already had all the tools and expertise, and now she had prepared notes about how to structure the individual groups, when and where they'd meet, and how they'd come together within the larger community network.

She'd even made the leap to her second lily pad: buying a domain name. This is what I call a "make it real" step. It's a small, low-stakes, sometimes simply symbolic action that takes something you're creating out of the hypothetical and into the actual. It's not important whether she ever ends up using this domain; it's about "making it real" by transforming it from an amorphous idea into something concrete for her brain and her INS to register as *real*.

At this point, Lyla and I had refined her Big Direction hypotheses into two very clear new ones.

Hypothesis #1: Spirituality + Divinity School

1. Research grad schools

2. _____

3. _____

4. _____

And so on.

Hypothesis #2: Building "How Are You Doing, Really?" Community/Business + Facilitating Women's Groups

1. Brainstorm vision for a second group

2. Buy domain name

3. _____

4. _____

And so on.

So the next part of the process was to observe and to ask what new lily pads were now emerging. We were incorporating the information from the previous aligned action and iterating upon it to determine the next warmer, Directionally right step. The key was continuing to take an action, *any* action.

Where is your curiosity leading you? What direction is warmer? What action holds the potential to get you more information and/or to continue moving the plot forward?

Again, there is never only one correct next action to choose. This is a common place where UFOAs get stuck, where perfection paralysis kicks in. UFOAs tend to want to find the absolute best, most perfect next action, to pick the unquestionably most ideal lily pad so that they can skip a few lily pads and leap ahead to being in divinity school and having launched a big, thriving community. No matter how big and brilliant your brain is, and I have no doubt that it is extremely big and brilliant, lily padding is *not* brain work. It's INS work. Your brain doesn't have the answers here, so don't let it take the reins. To repeat, in order to live Directionally, we need to be in the process of the unfolding, not in the outcome at the end of the unfolding.

So, first, take an action, *any* action. If this action doesn't get you the information you need, that's information in and of itself! This will still lead to the next lily pad. By definition, doing this well means refining as you go.

Second, recognize that your old Destinational thinking and your Fear Self are absolutely going to jump in to try to sabotage you at the first glimpse of change and uncertainty. You're going to feel uncomfortable. You're going to want off the lily pads and onto firm, predictable ground. I get it. And yet, the far better, ultimately more easeful and enjoyable approach is to get comfortable on the lily pads. If you skip the lily pads, you skip the fulfillment.

As far as divinity school, the next step that crystallized for Lyla was to organize a list of schools and programs that she was considering and to put all of their informational sessions on her calendar. Her job was simply to show up to the sessions and be on the lookout for emerging lily pads.

Her second hypothesis, the How Are You, Really? community, was a bit different. Building a business—building anything— Directionally is a distinctly different endeavor from building a business Destinationally. UFOAs assume that what comes first is the website, the catchy tagline, the logo, the branding, the professional headshots, and the complete business plan. But it's almost always more efficient and effective to begin with a minimum viable product (MVP), or the earliest, Directionally right version of a product that's functional and working well enough to "soft launch" to users and get feedback. This is sometimes called alpha or beta testing in tech launches, indicating that the creators know it's early and not fully baked. They expect the product to be buggy. It's a work in progress. We can have alpha testing and soft launches in our lives, too.

I've seen UFOAs spend months, even years, developing the infrastructure around the thing instead of iterating on the thing itself. This is yet another clever version of perfectionist procrastination and the Destinational Fear Self. When I was first building my coaching practice, I thought I needed to invest a lot of money in a beautiful website that articulated exactly who I was and what I was about and that spoke directly to "my ideal client" before I could coach even one person. But it was working with clients that helped me determine the people with whom I wanted to work and how best to articulate the kinds of work that I most wanted to do, which ultimately made for a much better, clearer, and more resonant message on my website than anything I could have come up with before I started doing the work itself.

Before we met and without knowing the full extent of what she was putting into motion, Lyla had launched the earliest version of her group and her business. So her next lily pad was a "soft launch" with a second group incorporating her earliest learnings. This entailed creating a very basic website to host the information, though she could have also done this in an email, and then sharing it with a small group of people. Each step was as easy and simple as possible.

Hypothesis #1: Spirituality + Divinity School

1. Research grad schools

2. Make a list of top schools + attend informational sessions

3. _____

4. _____

Hypothesis #2: Building "How Are You Doing, Really?" Community/Business + Facilitating Women's Groups

1. Brainstorm vision for a second group

2. Bought domain name

3. "Soft launch" of group two: build a very basic, info-only, work-in-progress website, and share invites

4. _____

The Aligned Action Formula

Okay, so what happens if you can't see any lily pads yet?

Sometimes, it's true that the first lily pad isn't so obvious or doesn't emerge right away, and we need to jump-start the process. This is neither good nor bad and means absolutely nothing about you and/or the viability of your hypothesis. And the solution is one of those remedies that's embarrassingly easy and obvious, like drinking a glass of water. We'd often prefer the answer to be bigger and harder and more complex, but I promise that this will dislodge just about any stuck lily pad.

Here is the foolproof five-step Aligned Action Formula:

1. Screenshot your mind.

2. Articulate the desire. (Say it out loud.)

3. Do some research on it. (Google it!)

4. Have a conversation.

5. Take an action, any action.

STEP ONE: Screenshot your mind. Every action starts with a "screenshot" of an idea. First, you have the idea, but then you must pay close enough attention to the idea to capture it; that's the only way to activate it. So often, the Fear Self intercepts and rejects any new, potentially disruptive idea before we can even consider it. We're not just talking about world-saving, life-altering, exceptionally brilliant, never-before-been-seen ideas. These can be any thoughts that feel warmer, especially ones that come to you repeatedly, from what you want to have for dinner to a hairstyle you want to try, a place you want to visit, a business you want to start, an industry you'd like to learn more about, or a vague sense of your Something Bigger.

I'm using the metaphor of the screenshot because it invokes the active and engaged way in which we want to work with our ideas here in Directional Living land. Screenshotting an idea is an intentional way of engaging with that thought, whereas simply "having" an idea is much more passive. To screenshot something—to actively press a button or the Ctrl + whatever keys on your keyboard—requires presence and awareness, which is what we want to cultivate within ourselves. Without a screenshot of an idea, we have nothing to put through the formula, nothing to activate and iterate on, so developing a practice of noticing and screenshotting your mind—taking yourself and your ideas seriously—is essential.

The good news is that you already know how to do this. Capturing is a big part of what we worked on in the last chapter in exploring your Big Direction—screenshotting even what seemed like the most outlandish or insignificant ideas and bypassing your Fear Self in order to take them seriously. This plugs right into where we left off in the last chapter, and for now, your Something Bigger hypothesis is a great step-one screenshot. This formula works for *any* idea or hypothesis you want to explore, big or small, not just those that derive from the more extensive Big Direction process in the last phase.

Let's explore an example of how this might play out in one of the other warmer ideas Lyla had in her Big Direction process: starting a podcast.

Imagine that Lyla's been having the same thought regularly for a while: *It would be so fun to have my own podcast.* Most of the time she dismisses this idea, ceding to her Fear Self: *That's a dumb idea. No one's interested in your lame podcast. There's nothing original about you or that idea. It's so cliché. Besides, you already have a big, successful career and people depending on you. You don't have time for anything else. Plus, you don't know anything about podcasting. That's not your strength.* And just like that, in a matter of seconds, her podcast idea dies a speedy death, never to be born. Poor podcast!

But since she's been tending to her True Self's thoughts, the next time the idea pops into her mind, she listens to it, honors it, and screenshots it: *It would be so fun to have my own podcast.*

Lyla's Idea: Start a podcast.

STEP TWO: Articulate the desire. Now Lyla articulates the desired hypothesis by saying it out loud to herself or writing it down, or both. Next, she says it to someone who cares about her. (Yes, her therapist or her beloved coach count.) Her current How Are You Doing, Really? group also definitely counts. If she's still a little sheepish about the idea, she can use humor and/or nonchalance: "I keep having this weird idea to start a podcast. Random, right?!" Now it's out in the world. *Woo-hoo!*

STEP THREE: Do some research on it. Today, this just means googling it. We have no excuses. This doesn't entail a field trip to the library and messing with a card catalog (for those of you old enough to remember such contraptions). Lyla could do it on the subway on her way home from dinner. Simply type "how to start a podcast." She only needs to read through the search results, go down the rabbit hole of the interwebs, and let the information just wash over her. Done.

Of course, you want to be discerning about what sources you trust. This isn't going to be the complete and final collection of information and everything you need to know, but it will generate new ideas, paths to consider, and questions to ask.

Lyla's Research Takeaways: There are classes that teach a step-by-step process for starting a podcast; a list of all the necessary equipment and tech.

STEP FOUR: Have a conversation. Next, Lyla needs to think of someone, anyone, who might have even an iota of information for her on this topic. She knows a few people who have podcasts, and she thinks she might have met a podcast editor at one point, too. She's been on a few podcasts and can email one or two of the hosts. Reach out—get some conversations on the calendar!

Sometimes you won't have a connection that's that direct or explicit. Maybe it means reconnecting with the sound technician you met at that birthday dinner. Or maybe your friend did a podcast interview that one time three years ago. Maybe you know an agent or a brand strategist who has a client with a podcast. This all counts.

STEP FIVE: Take an action, any action. Finally, take an action, any action. Steps two through four are designed to culminate in an action. After saying it out loud, doing some research, and having a relevant conversation or two, you now have more information than you started with. At this point, you're looking for a low-stakes microaction that you feel engaged in and excited about doing. As you know, there is no perfect action to take here. You will be able to take more actions later on. Pick one aligned action that feels warmer and Directionally right, then start. If you're feeling extra inspired, there is no rule against picking more, but one is all you need.

Some aligned action options for Lyla to consider next are:

- Listen to a variety of podcasts to get inspiration and ideas about what she might talk about in hers and how she'd like to structure it (interviews, themed solo episodes, etc.).

- Take a class on making a podcast.

- Compile a list of relevant resources to read/watch.

- Send a message to your favorite podcaster and ask if she can talk to them. (It doesn't matter if she never hears back. Maybe they'll respond, but if even if they don't, taking the action is the most important part.)

- Buy a piece of equipment from the list she researched and start practicing with it.

- Record a voice note of yourself talking about a topic of interest; this is for your ears only! See how she feels after.

Generally, some other great default actions of the low-stakes, high-activation sort for any idea you've screenshotted are: read a book, listen to a podcast, sign up for a class, take a field trip to an applicable location, buy something necessary for the project, find a symbolic physical reminder of your screenshot to keep it top of mind, or any action that can be scheduled and put on your calendar. And remember, there are many exploratory aligned actions that cost exactly zero dollars, so don't let your Fear Self turn limited funds into an excuse!

These five steps do not have to take a lot of time and effort, especially because you are calibrated and trued now. On any given day, this entire activation cycle could happen *before 9:00 a.m.*! (But you're not doing it wrong if it takes days or weeks instead.)

Once you've gone through the five-step process, then what? Back to step one with the next screenshot! Through the five steps, we move from the original screenshotted idea in step one to the *next idea,* which is spit out at the end of the fifth step based on all the new information we have obtained from steps two through four. This new idea then gets plugged back into step one for screenshotting.

For Lyla's podcast, maybe that last action is enrolling in an online workshop on podcast creation led by her favorite host, a workshop she didn't even know existed before completing these five steps. Next, she scans for a new Directionally right idea: maybe while she's taking the workshop, she starts thinking about pitching her concept to a potential corporate sponsor. She plugs *that*—pitching a sponsor—back into step one, first screenshotting the thought in her mind, then articulating her desire for a sponsored podcast (step two), researching some sponsors (step three), having a conversation about podcast sponsorship (step four), taking the resulting next aligned action (step five) . . . and so on. Wash, rinse, repeat.

These five steps are not one and done, check the box, arrive at your destination (because we don't do destinations anymore!). These activation cycles build on each other *Directionally.* Each activation cycle is like a paragraph in a chapter of a book: significant and meaningful in and of itself but also most powerful when set in the context of the whole.

Aligned Action Formula Checklist

1. Screenshot your mind.

- Idea: _____
  (Option: Insert a Big Direction hypothesis from the last phase.)

2. Articulate the desire. (Say it out loud.)

- To whom: _____

3. Do some research on it. (Google it!)

- Key learnings: _____

4. Have a conversation.

- With whom: _____

5. Take an action, any action.

- Next aligned action: _____

The EA

The hardest part of all this for us UFOAs is typically "letting go of control" and taking actions without expectation of specific results. This certainly was the case for me, and it is for most of my clients as well. For decades, we believed that our (perceived) ability to control—to influence and determine outcomes through planning and strategizing ten steps ahead and anticipating future events—was our defining superpower, *the* reason why we were successful and, simultaneously, our security blanket making us feel safe.

A lot of very wise spiritual people tell us to "surrender" and "let go." But what does that even mean? Surrendering can sound terrifying, even irresponsible! It seems like the opposite of assertiveness and accountability. Why would anyone want to disempower themselves like that? How can less control possibly yield better, more fulfilling results?

After I wrestled for years with this oft-repeated advice, it finally clicked for me: letting go of control is just *delegation*. This was something with which I had become very familiar in my corporate life and a concept I could intuitively grasp. Delegation is a smart and efficient skill that's part of effective management and leadership, which is something I could get behind. Delegation isn't passive; it's a proactive decision to assign specific oversight to an appropriate other. It's not an abdication of responsibility but rather a distributing of responsibility. In this way, delegation is letting go of full and complete control of the outcomes without "dropping the ball." It's not white-flag surrender, as in giving up and lying down. Instead, it's *active* surrender, as in a conscious and intentional, even strategic, choice to *allow*. There's a big difference between the feeling of *I've assigned this to someone else, and it is being taken care of* and *I'm letting this go and forgetting about it*, or just *I'm not going to try to control this anymore.*

You wouldn't delegate to just anyone, though. Imagine a truly outstanding executive assistant (EA), someone you trust so thoroughly that you can give them absolutely any task, vague or specific, big or small, and know beyond a shadow of a doubt that it will be taken care of with competence and grace and meticulousness—and *so much better* than you could have completed it yourself. If you have trouble imagining a human with this capability, imagine a nonhuman, artificially intelligent EA who is completely attuned to your unique needs.

This rare breed of trusted, wholly reliable EA is exactly the kind of support I've found helpful to envision when thinking about how to delegate all the bits and pieces that we encounter while making our way toward our Something Bigger. You could certainly delegate to "the universe" or to "universal intelligence" or to "a higher power" or to "Spirit" or to any other term that resonates for you in this context, and if that works for you, great! But sometimes such entities feel too abstract for our concrete UFOA brains to connect to. Personally, I've never been able to conjure a higher power to whom I could just "turn over" control. It always felt like a big scam. Now, I realize that "surrendering" to a flawless yet ultimately fictitious "EA" might sound just as far-fetched, but bear with me, and maybe give it a try, because, well, it's worked for many UFOAs.

Now, imagine that you've just hired your own personal EA. Consider your EA a sort of personified delegate from the universe. In the same way that it's helpful to personify our Fear Self and our True Self to help our tactical and practical brains concretize these concepts, it's useful to do the same with your EA character. Name your

EA if you like. Formulate an image of your EA. This EA is here to support and assist *you,* no one else. Your EA's job is to take on whatever tasks you delegate. This is your partner and advocate in your Big Direction, your aligned ambition, and your Directionally right actions, as well as in every concern, anxiety, problem, and HAYWALT. There is not a single thing that you cannot bring to your EA.

To make it even more tangible, try communicating with your EA directly. If you had a real-life, full-time assistant, what would you do? You might give your assistant daily briefings on the status of everything in your life and provide them with a to-do list, right?

I've found that a daily practice of writing "the EA email," in which you delegate anything and everything in your world that is delegable, can be quite effective in helping UFOAs let go of control and embrace active surrender. Many UFOAs even find it worthwhile to create an actual email alias for their EA (not kidding!), like MyEA@gmail.com, and to send an email every morning outlining their daily EA assignments and requests. But you can communicate with your EA in any way that feels good to you. Play around, try different things, and get creative with it!

In your daily briefings, assume that your EA has access to, or can get access to, information you don't have (like access to the higher video-game intelligence that knows all the forthcoming lily pads). Ask your EA for help. Ask your EA to take care of *anything* that causes you stress, that you don't know the answer to, and that you have questions about. This can be personal or professional and can be especially powerful when you are in the middle of the lily pad process. Maybe you're feeling stuck on what the next action is or with whom to have a conversation as part of the Aligned Action Formula. Ask your EA. Maybe you're trying to evaluate how much warmer or colder a specific choice is or how to address a particular HAYWALT. Ask your EA.

Keep in mind that there's nothing worse than a micromanager. The most crucial part of this process is trusting that whatever you've delegated is being taken care of and not meddling once you've assigned it! Here's an example of a daily EA briefing email from Lyla:

EA,

1. Can you help me figure out all the logistics for the 2nd group? Where should we meet? How many people is ideal? Who are the ideal participants? How long should the initial commitment be?

2. On that note, I'm feeling really unclear about how much I should be charging for my new groups. Can you do some research and let me know what's an optimal rate and also how to communicate this to my new clients effectively and confidently?

3. I want to keep enhancing my vision for my How Are You Doing, Really? group. Can you help me think through what might be the biggest, most aligned thing for this new business?

4. I'm so curious about divinity school. Can you help me assess if it's Directionally right for me? If so, which school? And what are the next steps?

5. Should I shut down my current consultancy entirely and hand it off to Carly? Or should I do a taper approach? Or part-time?

6. No urgency here, but I've been thinking about singing and how much I miss it ever since I did the Big Direction exercises. If it makes sense, would you look into singing lessons?

7. I'd like to start a daily writing practice and see where that takes me, but I'm having trouble finding (making?) time for this. Can you take a look at my calendar and block out times for me and help me figure out what the right cadence and routine is? And if I have an inner blindspot that's getting in the way and that I need to address, I'd like to know that, too. I want to make this a priority.

8. All those HAYWALTs I wrote out in the phase three work! There are still some that I need to rid myself of, and I'm stuck. Can you please help? Also, if there are any HAY-WALTs that I missed, please share!

9. My brother is really struggling right now. I want to help, but I don't know how. I'm not even sure if I can help, but it is really painful to watch him suffer. Can you check on him for me? Maybe talk to *his* EA and see if there is anything I'm not seeing that I can do to support him?

Keep me posted with any updates or leads!

Lyla

The EA practice works because it makes active surrender tangible and gives your brain somewhere and someone to delegate *to*, a place to deposit all these letting-go items. By giving you a co-creation partner, it allows you to experience what co-creation and letting go of results really *feels* like. Delegation to an actual human, such as a brilliantly competent EA whom you deeply, deeply trust and feel guided and supported by, is the closest analogy to what this experience, this posture, and this relationship to decision-making that we are going for in Directional Living feels like internally, which helps our brains to get on board with this concept more easily. When you're delegating to your EA, it doesn't feel like you are letting go of control (and therefore falling into a terrifying abyss of uncertainty) so much as it feels like you are wisely, proactively, and oh-so-efficiently assigning control elsewhere. Things are still "under control." You're just not the one in charge at the moment. This is much more palatable to the Fear Self.

This EA practice allows us to relinquish control "safely" so that we can live Directionally and experience our aligned success. It doesn't matter that no one is actually receiving this note or responding in-line. Just as drafting an angry email to someone who's hurt you can be effective even if you know you're never going to send it, there's an energetic shift that happens when you commit to this exercise. When we act *as if* we're delegating the next steps and they are officially off our plate, when we go through the motions of turning tasks over, our brains don't know the difference. We're sending our brains the message that they can stop trying to anticipate outcomes and ruminate on every possible future permutation of events, since things have now been delegated and are "under control." We're telling our brains that it's safe to release. Energetically, psychically, there's a change. It's then we discover that it actually doesn't feel so scary to let go of results and that it can even be a deep relief to stop trying to control outcomes.

The point here is also not about getting an actual reply, of course. The point is to practice being in "ready position"—the posture of co-creation, of letting go of results, of staying on our side of the net. The point is to be in conversation, to be in the asking, and to remember that this is a two-sided rally, not a solitary game.

But, still, you're probably wondering: *What happens after I delegate something to my EA? Because . . . the EA isn't real, right?*

While a human or AI EA would send you an actual email or

otherwise update you to let you know that it is your turn to jump in again and take a next action, with our version of the EA, you won't get a bulleted email response, obviously, but the answers *will* come to you. You'll get responses in the form of new ideas, new information, bits of inner knowing, and what some people call "downloads," or "intuitive hits." Your INS will announce your new coordinates and direction.

The idea here isn't that you delegate and then never touch the thing ever again; it's that you consciously practice releasing your viselike grip of control on everything in your life. And, even more so, it's that you recognize there are things—most things!—that you cannot control in the first place, no matter how brilliant and talented you are and no matter how hard you try, and that you experience knowing it is safe to do so. You give permission to your EA or the universe to take some of the next steps and then come back to you when it is your "turn" to get involved again and when you can do so productively and constructively. In fact, my suggestion is that you follow up with your EA each morning (or at whatever regular interval works for you) on the "open action items" from the day before and see if you have any more information or new intuitive ideas to screenshot. This way, you're keeping tabs on the progress and checking in without micromanaging.

Shortly after Lyla sent that email, for example, she stopped perseverating and ruminating on the answers to the questions she wrote out. She attended a seemingly unrelated networking event at a local flower shop just a few blocks from her home, and as soon as she walked in, she knew it was the perfect place for her to host her groups. After being in the space and securing the rates for use, she could easily envision exactly how many people should attend and what to charge. The "answer" presented itself.

A few days later, as she was putting out feelers and invitations for her next group, a friend introduced her to someone who she thought would be a great fit for the group, and it turned out that this woman was not only an ideal participant but also a voice and presence teacher. They decided to exchange services: private voice lessons for participation in the second How Are You Doing, Really? group. Another answer!

For months, Lyla had been sending books and articles and suggestions to her brother in an effort to help him with his mental health struggles, but none of it was working. In fact, it seemed to make things worse. After she delegated this to her EA, though, she stopped trying so hard and doing so much and waited until she heard a different suggestion. It was at this point that it occurred to her to share with me what was going on with her brother and how it was affecting her—to have a conversation, à la step four in the Aligned Action Formula. I offered that perhaps the best thing she could do to help him was to actually focus less on "fixing" him and more on taking care of *herself* in these circumstances. I shared some resources including some groups she herself could attend that focused on the family members, not the person suffering. Her relationship with her brother started to change after that.

This isn't some water-into-wine, laws-of-physics-defying miracle stuff. Obviously, it was Lyla herself who took action—talking to the flower shop's owner about renting the space, initiating a conversation about exchanging services with the voice coach, and confiding in me and then utilizing the resources I offered. She is the one "making it real." Could all these things have happened even if she hadn't "collaborated" with her EA? Perhaps, but pre-EA, she would have been much more likely to obsessively research event spaces, contact everyone she knew for suggestions, and make a decision that was out of alignment three weeks earlier, by doing something like picking a too-expensive, fine-but-not-ideal location just to get something to happen out of confusion and fear and urgency. In other words, she would have tried to exert control and "make" the outcomes happen, and in doing so, she may never have even gotten to this more aligned, Directionally right event space that delighted her and allowed her to envision the other details of the evolving group in a new way.

For our purposes, we might narrate this as equivalent to a human or AI EA sending a message saying, "What about this flower shop space? Take a look, talk to the owner, and see what you think!" Or an email saying, "I found someone who might be a great voice coach for you and won't require a huge investment or commitment," along with a website link and contact info. That's what this Directional Living experience *feels* like. We continue to co-create and "rally" in dialogue with our EAs, not bow out entirely. Of course, we are the ones who take actions in the tangible, 3D world of reality, but preferably only when our EAs come back to us with some new information, downloads, or prompts.

When we stop staring at the empty spaces in front of us where we think lily pads should be, willing them to emerge (which is what most of us spend our lives trying to do, though it most certainly doesn't work), we free ourselves up to *allow* them to reveal themselves. Our job is just to be on the lookout and to take the steps when they do appear.

I also don't want to overpromise immediate results when it comes to each and every thing you bring to your EA. Again, this isn't magic and miracles, and it's not wishful thinking. Some things will take years to unfold or will never happen in the way you imagine, and it will take practice to accept that what you may have previously envisioned is simply not Directionally right for you. The work is about supporting ourselves in getting out of our own way so that we can live our most aligned and Directionally right lives.

The EA exercise requires a bit of a mental leap, I know, but it's one I have found to be supremely effective in my own life, as well as in the lives of my clients. And it's also just one way to conceptualize this dynamic approach. Not every exercise will work for every single person, so if this doesn't land for you, don't worry about it! Maybe "allowing" and "trusting the unfolding" is very easy for you, so you don't need something like this. What I can say is that I have never worked with someone who has decided to engage with the EA concept and not found it transformative in some way.

Where Did Lyla's Lily Pads Lead Her?

Lyla did go to a bunch of info sessions for divinity schools. They were definitely warmer, but she'd gotten honest with herself that as much as she'd wanted that to be The Path, when it came to actually applying, that just didn't feel like the next Directionally right step. She was disappointed, and she didn't understand why it didn't feel light and right and like a "Hell yes." She felt stuck, and the next lily pad wasn't clear at the time. So she said it out loud, wrote to her EA, did some more research, and had some more conversations.

One of those chats was with her rabbi, whom you might recall she'd noted in her Big Direction process as someone she'd wanted to shadow. It was during their discussion that the next lily pad emerged: she would go to rabbinical school. This was absolutely shocking to her, as this was far from the path she'd envisioned for herself and far from how "the world" saw her. She had some judgment and some resistance. And yet she didn't have any doubt that this was the next Directionally right step and the way to her Something Bigger. And so that's what she did.

After Lyla decided on rabbinical school, the next steps seemed so obvious to her. We revisited her exercises and realized that all her Big Direction hypotheses braided together here: spirituality/philosophy, counseling/mentorship, community/group facilitation. Now she spends her days studying and discussing spirituality and theology. She's building and leading her own community. She's counseling people privately. She's facilitating sacred life-milestone ceremonies. She even gets to sing as part of her job! It wasn't a starting over, as she feared. It's clear that everything she did before, all her past work in building and developing communities, prepared her more fully to step up and into this new life.

We can't forget about her How Are You Doing, Really? groups. She launched a second and a third and, eventually, a tenth. She developed a curriculum and trained other facilitators. It grew into a thriving business and community serving hundreds of women whom she adored. She kept running it while she was in school, which not only helped her to pay for school but also felt like an aligned creative counterbalance to her studies. She's had acquisition offers, which she's considering, but none of them have felt Directionally right, *yet*.

Many UFOAs have a moment like Lyla did about rabbinical school, where it feels like you snap into your life so fully that you can almost hear it click. Suddenly, it's hard to believe that there was ever a time when you didn't have that level of knowing. This next lily pad step, whatever it is, becomes something that you cannot *not* do, even if it doesn't make any "logical" sense to you and you can't see where it's leading. It feels so true and so clear and so real and so *definitive* that it almost feels like a memory of the future. And it is, in a way. It's a remembering of your True Self, of your alignment, of your personal Something Bigger.

That's the thing with lily padding: the big leaps will feel like small leaps by the time you get there. There's no cliff jumping required in Directional Living. Whether it's a milestone step like going to graduate school, quitting the career trajectory you thought was forever, getting married, or buying a house, or a smaller step like attending an information session, updating your résumé, going on a first date, or touring open houses, the distance will always be about the same—that is to say, manageable. It will simply be the next most aligned action.

For your truest, most aligned results, let go of them—this is the paradox at the center of Directional Living. Your most fulfilled life comes from controlling less, not more. Allow more, will less. The less you impose your agenda, the more aligned—the truer—your life will be. The less focus you give to the outcome, the more fulfilling the process and the result will be.

It's counterintuitive but it makes sense, too. It's like asking a leading question instead of an open-ended one—you will probably get a less true answer. In the scientific method approach to life, it's like manipulating an experiment to confirm your hypothesis rather than allowing an experiment to yield results in order to then evaluate your hypothesis. You might pull it off and create the result you planned for, but it won't yield true insight.

Ultimately, it's our relationship with control—how much we think we have and how much we try to exert—that differentiates Destinational Living from Directional Living, and therefore unfulfillment from fulfillment. The questions for the Underfulfilled Overachiever, then, are: How badly do you want to find fulfillment and meaning and purpose, and a life you love living that feels truly like *your* life? How badly do you want freedom? Relief? Peace? Ease? Joy? Because all of that is on the other side of ditching the control tactics of Destinational Living. The irony, of course, is that we're afraid of letting go of something that we never actually had in the first place. The control we seek is, and has always been, an illusion.

Lyla's almost done with rabbinical school now, at which point she'll find herself at another crossroads. Does she want to be a congregational rabbi or apply her education and expertise in some other way? I asked her about her most aligned ambitions and whether a new hypothesis for her evolving Big Direction had emerged yet. "Not yet," she told me, "but I'm delightfully and uncharacteristically unstressed about the whole thing." Then, with a smile, she added, "After all, I only need to see as far as the headlights in front of me, and I can make the whole trip that way."

The Directional Living Movement

Imagine yourself one year from today. Imagine that you are 100 percent your full-on, Directionally right True Self on your path of aligned ambition. What does that look like? How do you know? Act as if you're watching yourself in a day-in-the-life clip; what tips you off that you are fully trued?

Now, let's also pretend there's some amazing new infrared technology that can scan your emotions and tell you what you're feeling internally as well. Take a moment here. Notice the external or internal indicators that would demonstrate your being exactly where you're supposed to be in your life, living in your full aliveness. What do you notice about this person? (Watch out for your Fear Self trying to hijack this!)

That experience of being exactly where you are supposed to be, doing exactly what you are meant to be doing, that ideal state of ease and purpose and presence and joy and authenticity? That is wholeness, the state of alignment and integrity, and it's the result of consistent Directional Living. There's no F-ache here. This is where fulfillment lives. See if you can tap in to that feeling and really grab ahold of it—bottle it so you can refer back to it.

Wholeness is different from perfect. It is a sense of completeness, yes, but it is not about being conclusively complete or "finished." It's about being Directionally complete—complete for wherever you are in the context of your larger Directional evolution. It's the experience of fully inhabiting your True Self, with all the messiness, all the layers and complexity and contradiction, of fully inhabiting the totality of who you are and who you are becoming. It's being in—gasp!—your full humanity.

When we UFOAs think we need perfection, what we are really craving is the 360-degree clarity that comes from the feeling of wholeness. Wholeness is what "perfect" would look like if it were Directional, not Destinational. Perfection is fixed—it limits you—whereas wholeness is expansive—it lets you evolve.

Wholeness is also different from happiness or feeling good all the time. Your Directionally right will, at times, require you to confront painful things about yourself and the world, and still, in these moments (especially in these moments), you are whole.

Wholeness is often two things at once. It's both/and. You can be in wholeness while your Fear Self is also throwing a temper tantrum. You can be in wholeness and still have HAYWALTs you're working through. You can be in wholeness while in the middle of multiple cycles of Directional iterations. In fact, I hope you find yourself in all of these states of wholeness! They are evidence that you are continuing to live Directionally, iterating, adapting, and evolving as you go.

Wholeness is the result of the Directional Living process we've gone through in this book. But, I hate to break it to you, this process is not a one-shot deal. That doesn't mean you need to sit down with this program and follow it to a T many times over, though that's not a bad idea—I do it in full annually myself! You may choose to revisit an exercise or a section here and there, as needed. However you decide to utilize the content of this book moving forward, though, you will need to call on each of these phases many more times in your Directional Life.

There's always more to uncover about the ways your old, inherited Destinational patterns show up. At some point, you'll want to check in with the Fulfillment Test and comb through a decision for the Four Omens in the first phase. Sometimes a big fat metaphorical magnet will come and mess with the compass of your Inner Navigation System, and you'll want to do a True Self reboot; here the tools of the Align phase will guide you.

And while the nature of deHAYWALTing is that it's an ongoing process, if you're doing it regularly, you may not need to do a big HAYWALT purge very often (or ever again). But there will come an occasion when you need to reach for even more courage in order to release something that isn't aligned for you anymore. These practices will be there for you.

You're going to take detours. You'll fall back into a blind ambition trap. And you'll need to reorient to your Big Direction as we did in phase four. You're going to get impatient at times, and you're going to think, *Enough with this "let go of results" shit.* You're going to fall back on brute-force tactics and try to make things happen again, and . . . it's not going to work, because it never does. So you'll revisit the Iteration phase and immerse yourself in lily pads and the Aligned Action Formula.

Remember the Principle of Exposure? No matter how much or how little you feel like you've "done" or "accomplished" with this book, I assure you that you've absorbed way more than you realize.

And I promise, you'll surprise yourself at some point when some phrase or analogy or story or exercise or framework pops into your head and sheds light on a new situation.

You don't have to fear getting lost or stuck anymore. Because if, and *when*, that happens, you'll know what to do. You literally have the manual. This process lives in you now. It's yours. You will know where to begin again.

This process will grow with you if you let it. If you come back to the work in this book tomorrow or a year from now or five years from now, your experience will be completely different. You'll hear things differently. The learnings will land in new ways. The phases will resonate more, or less, depending on where you are and what you need to hear. There will always be something here for you.

This is radical work. Unlearning everything you've been taught and doing the opposite is profound. It's revolutionary to choose what feels true to you instead of what you've been told is true. It's radical to co-create instead of control, to center curiosity and joy as the building blocks of your life, to insist on "becoming who you truly are." Dedicating yourself to what you want and what you love, building a life that is uniquely yours, and listening to your own Inner Navigation System instead of the outsourced consensus of Destinationalism is radical. Saying "I don't know" to the question of where you will be in ten years while existing in our current Destinational world is radical. Choosing yourself is radical. As AOC said about refusing to decide on her future political aspirations: "If I have too many [Destinational] ambitions, I can't be brave now."

Directional Living is the real "radical self-care," beyond bath bombs and face masks and massages; it's creating a life so aligned for you that you don't need to escape it. The caring-est self-care you can do is seek wholeness.

Directional Living is inherently hopeful, and that's a radical stance to take, too. It's a belief in our individual and collective potential. It's a willingness to participate in the reimagining of what's possible and in the building of that new future. It's a growth mentality, not a fixed one. When we stop focusing on the future, we enable real evolution and growth. When we focus ourselves on staying in our own alignment, we are caring for, growing with, and benefiting those around us. It's not just the truest form of self-care—it's community care, too.

And when you start sharing more creative ideas and innovative solutions from your True Self, achieving more less anxiously, people notice and want to join you. They will want to know what your secret is. I've had clients report that they've been asked if they got Botox, went on a meditation retreat, got fitter, or were doing something new in bed. You'll be a more valuable employee, teammate, and collaborator, which will likely correspond to more lucrative opportunities. You'll be a more present and authentic spouse and friend and parent and child and human, which will likely correspond to deeper and richer relationships.

The work of Directional Living is about you, and it's about way more than you.

When you make this foundational shift to Directional Living, it sets off a chain reaction. When you stop letting your Fear Self run your life and show up as your True Self instead, you give others permission to do the same. When you stop attempting to control outcomes and instead embrace an experimental, launch-and-iterate approach, others will be inspired. When you stop relying on external guidance and instead lead with your own Inner Navigation System, it will change the dynamic of every environment you're in—in your family, your friend group, your office, your community. You'll be one less voice contributing to the chorus of "shoulds" and enforcing Destinational norms for those in your orbit. You'll become an influential example of what else is possible. And that matters.

It's radical to realize that when you're living as your True Self, what is in your highest good is also in the highest good of everyone around you. The most powerful way to impact your community is to be here, doing this, and committing to living Directionally, guided by your own trued Inner Navigation System.

In Directional Living, all boats rise with the tide, as the expression goes. When we operate from the understanding that we each have our own bespoke, most aligned path and our own personal navigational instructions to follow that are designed for us and no one else, we know there's plenty of room for everyone to thrive.

Baked into Directional Living is difference and true diversity. Directional Living can't coexist with the over/under philosophy embedded in many of the "isms" that plague us today—sexism, racism, ableism, ageism, classism, heterosexism, nationalism, even late-stage capitalism, to name a few.

What would it look like if we all lived Directionally—if this were our dominant cultural paradigm? What if we were all running around whole and aligned and fulfilled? If none of us were living under the tyrannical rule of the shoulds and instead living fully expressed, True Self–led lives?

Imagine if we parented Directionally rather than Destinationally. There'd be no perfect parenting, only aligned parenting for your particular child(ren) and your particular family, according to your True Self's guidance. What if children inherited Directional Living by default? What if they grew up trusting themselves and their own embodied, inner sense of direction, following their curiosity and honoring their joy to become who they really are, all without having to get it "right" or know exactly where they're going?

Can you imagine what it would be like if everyone was doing the work in the world that they were uniquely well suited to do instead of what they thought they "should" do? The innovation and the creativity in all sectors that this would spark—in arts, in tech, in government, in business. The cultural landscape would be so much richer and more vibrant. There would be so much less unnecessary suffering; mental health would drastically improve.

What would it look like to live in a Directional world? A world where our workplaces and our education system and our civic institutions were Directional and trued?

If every UFOA started living Directionally, there'd be a Directional movement of sorts. No great collective organizing needed. Just each of us, in our own lives, recalibrating our Inner Navigation Systems, following our True Self's guidance, aligning with our Big Direction, and living into our Directionally right. It's the epitome of the truism "Think globally, act locally." If we each tended to our own UFOA recovery, our own wholeness, however imperfectly, the impact would be far-reaching.

This work doesn't belong to me alone. It's not "mine." Or yours. It's ours. From one Underfulfilled Overachiever to another, this is your invitation to the Directional Living movement. It's already begun. Commit to yourself. Choosing yourself is hard, but not choosing yourself, turning away from your True Self day after day, is harder and far more painful. Join us.

This book needs you. It's up to you, my fellow Underfulfilled Overachiever, to put all these ideas into practice and make Directional Living real in the world.

Acknowledgments

Let me paint you a picture. It's 5:00 a.m. in the dark and I'm up to work before the baby wakes. This book is due (like really, really due) today and this is my last section to write. It's been four years since I began this book project—I'd estimate that I've worked on it at least 90 percent of the days in that time—and I'm afraid I may be out of words. And yet, somehow these pages come pouring out of me, and to my surprise, so do the tears.

It's not lost on me that I start this book on a scene where I'm crying in the dark, and now I'm crying in the dark again, as I finish it. I'm struck, once again, by just how far I have come, and how unrecognizable this life, and this self, would be to that bathroom floor version of me of ten-plus years ago. I am so grateful for her, that twenty-nine-year-old, who was so scared, and then so brave. I wish I could tell her it's all worth it. This life I have now is better than anything she could have imagined.

I truly can't believe how lucky I have been, and how privileged, to have benefited from such extraordinary support on this book and in my life.

I have the most aligned trifecta of women responsible for getting this thing out in the world: my agent, Mel Flashman; my editor, Emily Wunderlich; and my bonus editor, Victoria Loustalot. All three of you "got" what I was trying to do with this book project immediately and were there to guide me every time I got lost, which was often.

Mel, thank you for expanding my vision of what is possible for this book. With you in my corner, I've continuously felt so confident that everything is unfolding exactly as it should, and that is a rare and incredible gift.

Emily, you have been such a steady and patient hand in this process, and this book's biggest advocate since it was still just fragments of a newsletter. Thank you for giving this book a home.

Victoria, as I've told anyone who will listen, working with you has been like watching the best magic trick you've ever seen. How you took my two full-length roughest of rough drafts and helped me turn them into a real, live, coherent, readable book is a total mystery to me. I'm in awe and forever grateful.

To the whole Viking/Penguin Life and Janklow & Nesbit teams, there's so much that happens behind the scenes that I don't even know about, and that's a testament to how well you do your jobs. Thank you for taking this book and "making it real."

To each of my clients, thank you for letting me into your life and teaching me everything I know about UFOAs and how we can recover. This Directional process wouldn't exist without you. You have changed me, and you have made my life infinitely richer. It's such a cliché, but it's a cliché for a reason—it's the honor of my life to have supported you in whatever way I have.

AOC, thank you for letting me share your story—it has been the vehicle for so many UFOAs to find this work, and for that I am immensely grateful. The way you practice Directional Living in your life is beautiful.

To all my teachers and all the thinkers who came before me, many of whom I've included in the reading list in the appendix, thank you for your ideas and your wisdom and for sharing your work with the world. I followed my curiosity to your work and it revived me and reminded me of who I am. Thank you for informing and influencing and inspiring my thinking into what would become Directional Living.

Virginia Heffernan, thank you for believing in my work before there was even work to believe in. You've been workshopping this with me from day one and your brilliance is baked into everything I do. Without you, I'm pretty sure none of this—this book, these ideas, my coaching practice—would exist. More importantly, I'm not sure I would exist, at least not in any sane, aligned, or recognizable form. You've made Directional Living and living Directionally so much more fun.

Susanmerrie Hellerer, my soul (aunt-)friend, thank you for seeing me so completely, and always being the person to whom I can go when I'm in need of calibration. Your imagination for what is possible for my life saved me. And, together with Stephen Milgrim, thank you for being my second home and soft place to land since the beginning.

To my parents, Chris and Mark, thank you for loving me unconditionally. I have never once doubted that I am loved, and everything else in my life is possible because of that truth. Growing up with lawyers as parents, I became pretty good at "making a case" for things. You have many stories about my always asking, "Why?" to the nth degree and constructing arguments against systems and rules that didn't make sense to me, especially yours. Well, at least it wasn't all for naught! I think all my whys and case-building and arguing against systems were just practice for this book. It's impossible to enumerate all the ways that you have supported me and contributed to my life, so for now, suffice it to say thank you for teaching me how to think critically, always valuing my ideas and honoring my curiosity. I got very lucky landing you as parents.

To my sister, Caitlin, thank you for being my coaching guinea pig, even though this is probably news to you! Little did you know, when I strategically selected the movie *Ladybugs* when you were refusing to play soccer (which turned into an epic soccer career, by the way), or when we played the earliest alpha version of warmer-colder decision-making when you were deciding what college to go to that day in Central Park, that I was always experimenting on you! You're the reason I knew how powerful it could be to have a thought partner in life decision-making, to have someone "hold space" for you and to calibrate and interpret your Inner Navigation System with you. But my biggest thank-you is that, even in the darkest of days, I have never felt completely alone in the world because I have you.

To my daughter, Mara, I still can't believe I get to write those words. You will be one year old when this comes out, and it took just about as long for you to arrive in the world as it did for this book to. By no plan of my own, one of the most interesting things about the past few years is that two of my greatest (aligned) ambitions were in process of becoming at the same time: this book and you. As a result, on the way to having you, I was on the ultimate tour of the lessons of Directional Living—letting go of control, allowing, trusting the timing, co-creating, deHAYWALTing, lilypadding, taking aligned action, living by just the headlights—at the very same time I was attempting to articulate them to share with others, and this book is so much better for it. I can't wait to support you in uncovering your own Directionally right, Big Directions, and aligned ambition. My wish for you is to grow up in a world where Directional Living is the only thing you know, and Destinational Living is like an old dusty relic way of thinking that I have to explain to you like a rotary phone.

To my partner, Andy Romig, I couldn't imagine a more supportive partner. I realized just now that I've spent over half of our relationship working on this book. When I said I needed to go live in the woods alone for a few months and write, you said, "Go for it!" and took a bus to visit on weekends. When I said I'd need to do less income-generating work to focus on the book, you said, "We'll figure it out!" More recently, when my final edit was due while we had a newborn, you said, "Go write—I've got the baby." You celebrated every single milestone with me, from selling the book to getting some word or other right, and the first five thousand words to turning in the first manuscript (and the final one and every other one in between). And then, you led me through the most masterful and gorgeous edit, so good that when we were done, I fell in love with my own work all over again, and this book for the first time. I love you and I choose you.

To Andy and Mara (and Gussy the cat), you are my forever Directionally right.

To you, the readers of this book, and all the Underfulfilled Overachievers out there, thank you for taking this work and making it your own, bringing it into your worlds, and sparking a movement.

Additional Resources

Exercises, Prompts, and References

Contents

Resources for Phase II—Align

Cheat Sheet: Your Fear Self vs. True Self Legend

	Fear Self	True Self
	Universal References	
Approach	Destinational	Directional
Goal	to survive	to thrive
Language	Four Omens; fear	nonverbal; alignment
Feels like	colder; hard and heavy; resistance	warmer; light and right; ease
Sounds like	words and justifications; logic	absence of verbal logic
Lives in	mind	body/sensations
Results in	blind ambition; unfulfillment; F-ache	aligned ambition; fulfillment; no F-ache
	Your Personal References	
Name (if other than Fear/ True Self)		
Reference/ shortcut	(e.g., Dr. Dick)	(e.g., Maine)
Your sensations	(e.g., ick)	(e.g., yay)

Cheat Sheet: Detecting Your Fear Self Process

As with Allegra in the Align phase, if you're trying to make a decision and are having trouble discerning the most aligned path, here's a step-by-step process to reliably smoke out your Fear Self.

What are all the reasons why you believe you cannot actually choose what you strongly suspect is your True Self choice? And/or why "should" you choose the other option?

Option A:

_____

_____

_____

_____

Option B:

_____

_____

_____

_____

1. THINKING MIND (BRAIN) OR SENSING MIND (BODY)?

Is there a robust verbal explanation or justification? (In other words, did you write a bunch of stuff above?) Circle one.

Yes = Fear Self

No = True Self

2. WARMER-COLDER INS ASSESSMENT

a) Pick one core statement from the above explanation.

_____

_____

_____

b) Run this statement through your INS by doing the following:

"Try on" this statement in your mind and hold it for a moment until you can get a sense of how it feels in your body. Refer back to your legend on page 108 if you need to, and practice toggling back and forth between your warmer and colder references.

What does this statement feel like in your body?
What sensations do you notice?
(No explanations, only sensations!)

_____

_____

Is it warmer or colder? Light and right or hard and heavy?
Circle one.

Colder/hard and heavy = Fear Self
Warmer/light and right = True Self

If you like, apply the same process with the other statements on the previous page for confirmation.

3. THE FULFILLMENT TEST AND THE FOUR OMENS

Refer to your argument and go through it (maybe with a highlighter!) to look for each of the Four Omens. If you catch one of them, categorize it in the appropriate space below.

Omen #1: Obligation (the "shoulds")

KEY QUESTIONS: *What "should" I do here [according to others]? What would others advise?*

KEY INDICATORS: *"should," "should not," "supposed to"*

_____

_____

_____

_____

TO CHALLENGE: *Says who?*

_____

_____

Omen #2: Objectivity ("objective" logic and strategy)

KEY QUESTION: *What's the objectively "right," smartest, and/or most strategic move?*

KEY INDICATORS: *"logical," "I think," "right," "smartest," "best," "most strategic," "the most sense"; superlatives*

_____

_____

_____

_____

TO CHALLENGE: *Who says?* and *According to whom?*

TO CHALLENGE: *Smarter, better, and most strategic for whom?* and *According to what criteria?*

Omen #3: Optics

KEY QUESTIONS: *How will it look? How will it be perceived? What will it say about me?*

KEY INDICATORS: *"people will think . . . ," "it will look like I . . ."*

TO CHALLENGE: *Who, exactly, will think this? Does that person matter to you?*

About these faceless "people," you can also ask:

TO CHALLENGE: *Do I know with certainty that this is what "they" will think?*

TO CHALLENGE: *Is there another possible way that people could interpret my choice?*

TO CHALLENGE: *What's one other possible interpretation that's closer to the truth?*

_____

_____

_____

Omen #4: Outcomes

KEY QUESTIONS: *What will this get me? How will this advance me?*

KEY INDICATORS: *if-then statements; future tense; "so that"*

_____

_____

_____

TO CHALLENGE: *Can I know with certainty that this outcome will happen?*

_____

_____

TO CHALLENGE: *What's one other way this could turn out?*

_____

_____

_____

TO CHALLENGE: *What happens in the meantime? What will the process be like?*

_____

_____

_____

Final Tally

(Circle one in each line based on your results so far.)

1. THINKING MIND (BRAIN) OR SENSING MIND (BODY)?

Fear Self   True Self

2. WARMER-COLDER INS ASSESSMENT

Fear Self   True Self

3. FOUR OMENS

Obligation: Fear Self   True Self

Objectivity: Fear Self   True Self

Optics: Fear Self   True Self

Outcomes: Fear Self   True Self

Results:

If *any* of the above are "Fear Self," then it's likely a Fear Self position, and you want to exclude it from your decision-making.

If three or more of the above are "Fear Self," then it's very likely a Fear Self position, and you want to exclude it from your decision-making.

If five or more of the above are "Fear Self," then it's extremely likely a Fear Self position, and you want to exclude it from your decision-making.

If none of the above are "Fear Self," then congrats! You're in the clear and it's a sound and aligned basis for your decision!

Tips and Tricks—Identifying the Fear Self

Four More Fear Self "Tells"

In addition to the Four Omens, there are a few other common Fear Self communication tactics and key words that the Fear Self loves to use and that give it away.

1. The "Toos"

Any time you find yourself thinking that an idea is too much of something, or you yourself are too much of something, that's the Fear Self talking. If something is Directionally right for you, then it's not "too" anything, so this isn't language that the True Self uses. It sounds like:

"It's too hard/easy."
"I'm too old/young."
"It's too expensive."
"It's too much time."
"I'm too female."
"I'm too risk-averse."

2. Scarcity and Not-Enoughness

Scarcity is the opposite of the "toos," and any argument that is based on scarcity or not-enoughness, no matter how logical and responsible it sounds, is your Fear Self fearing. It might be true that you don't have enough experience or enough money to do something in particular, or at least not yet, but that doesn't mean there isn't a step that can't be taken in that direction. A path to saving, perhaps, or a scholarship, none of which you'll explore if you let your Fear Self squash the idea right off the bat. The Fear Self uses scarcity to justify shutting the whole thing down. It sounds like:

> *"I'll never find enough clients to support myself if I start my own consultancy."*
>
> *"I don't have enough experience to open a gallery."*
>
> *"I don't have enough money to go to that coding bootcamp."*
>
> *"I don't have enough tenure at this company to ask to work on that new project (that I'm so excited about and very qualified for)."*
>
> *"I'm not smart enough to be a great professor or charismatic enough to be a great leader or nurturing enough to be a good mother or pretty enough to be in a great relationship."*

3. Exceptionalism and "Compare and Despair"

When you compare yourself with others and feel like crap about yourself, that's the "scarcity" voice, just in comparative form. Exceptionalism is the voice that tells you you're "the only one" and the exception to what is possible. If you think you're the exception to the rule, or if any part of your decision-making rationale is based on comparison with others, it's very unlikely to be True Self thinking. It sounds like:

> *"Everyone else has a 'life purpose' and a 'passion,' but it doesn't exist for me."*
>
> *"Everyone except me has ten thousand followers and that 'swipe up' function. I might as well quit."*

"I'll never be as successful as Oprah, so what is the point of even trying?"

"He's been at this longer than I have, so I'll never be as successful as he is."

4. Urgency

Experiencing urgency around life deadlines, feeling behind on life, getting sucked into the culture of immediacy (hi, email and text and Slack!), and falling prey to hustle culture are all Fear Self tactics. If it feels urgent, it's not likely to be coming from your True Self. I love the idea behind the Eisenhower Matrix to bust this one (barring any true emergencies): *The urgent are not important, and the important are never urgent.* Urgency sounds like:

"I have to be married by thirty or . . . I'll never get married, because all the good ones will be taken."

"I have to get promoted THIS quarter or . . . I will never get promoted."

"I must become a VP within two years or . . . I'll have to change careers."

"I need to be on the Forbes '30 Under 30' list or . . . my career is doomed."

"If I don't finish my dissertation this year, then I should just drop out."

"I'm behind in life, and I'll never catch up."

Tips and Tricks—Quick and Easy
Fear Self–Slaying Techniques

Sometimes the Fear Self gets really loud, especially, counterintuitively, the closer we get to making our most aligned decision. When this happens, it can feel impossible to hear the True Self through the Fear Self's distortions. This is when some additional tools and support can help us get trued and aligned.

Here are some quick and simple Fear Self–slaying tricks to pull out whenever you find yourself under Fear Self attack or just need a little amplification of your True Self voice. In other words, here's your new anti-anxiety prescription.

Physical postures: These are known as "inversions" in yoga, and they work to calm the Fear Self response, because no human body in real and serious physical danger does an inverted posture; this signals to the Fear Self that all is well, you are safe, and it can relax, which in turn makes it easier to hear your True Self.

- **Legs-up-a-wall:** Lie on your back with your legs up against a wall for five to ten minutes (or longer, or whatever you've got!); try it daily—it feels amazing!

- **Forward fold:** Stand or sit bent over your legs, letting your head and arms hang for a few minutes.

Bilateral stimulation exercise: simple EMDR movement technique.

- Grab an item (doesn't matter what—a pen, a hair elastic, your smartphone) and pass it back and forth between your hands across the midline of your body.

Physical movement: "Move a muscle, change a thought."

• Move your body in any way, shape, or form. This "completes the cycle" of a Fear Self stress response. Take a walk, run a quick errand, do some gentle stretching, go to the bathroom, have a solo dance party in your living room, whatever! This can be fitness exercise, but it doesn't have to be. It can be much easier and quicker than that.

The anti–Fear Self writing practices (can be daily, or as needed):

• **The Presence Practice:** This is a super-effective Fear Self slayer because fear and gratitude/presence cannot coexist in the brain. The Presence Practice is my take on a gratitude list—but better. (If you're eye-rolling at "gratitude list" right now, I get it. I did, too, at first, but humor me. Try it out and just see how much less anxious you start to feel.) It's ten things—the smaller, the better—that happened in only the last twenty-four hours and, most importantly, triggered a feeling of deep appreciation. None of the broad-stroke gratitude "shoulds" like "I'm grateful to be alive"—unless you felt a particularly strong sense of being grateful for all of life on that day—but more like drinking that delicious cup of coffee, wearing your favorite shoes, or texting with your sister about something funny. We want to list things that you actually appreciated or delighted in, not attempt to convince yourself of things that you *should* be grateful for, which is what most of us UFOAs do in a gratitude list to try to make ourselves feel something we believe we "should" feel (yes, the Omens are everywhere!), instead of noticing and collecting what we're actually experiencing. Maybe you can only come up with two at first, and maybe it's the same two things every day, but with practice, you will notice more and more of these presence moments, and it will enhance your relationship with your True Self.

Rules of the Presence Practice List:

1. There must be ten presences (or ten times that you practice presence in that day)—no more, no less.

2. Write down only things that are from the last twenty-four hours.

3. Nothing is too small. In fact, the smaller, the better!

- **The Possibility Practice:** This is also an incredibly effective Fear Self–slaying technique because possibility and abundance override fearful feelings of exceptionalism and scarcity. This time, think of ten things that could go very, very right today. Small is great; crazy and "out there" is better! A good way to start is just by going through your day and imagining the most extraordinary result of each thing.

  - This works by counteracting the majority of our thoughts that are negative, focused on scarcity and amplifying our fears. In this practice, we're applying the saying "Wherever you put your attention grows" and redirecting our attention to strengthening the thoughts that are actually useful, authentic, and forward-thinking.

Take an action, any action: *Action is the antidote to fear.*

- This is the last step of the Aligned Action Formula from phase five. Find any aligned, "warmer" action at all, no matter how small, to break the Fear Self paralysis. This includes any step among those in the Aligned Action Formula checklist.

Feelings vs. facts: a two-column quickie exercise

- Draw a line down the middle of a piece of paper, à la a pros-and-cons list.

- On one side, write out all the *feelings* you have, no matter how petty or cringey they might seem to you.

- On the other, outline the most objective, simplistic version of the facts that you can.

- Compare! See how and where your Fear Self is driving the narrative and what another perspective you could take is.

Feelings	Facts
• Scared I'm getting fired • Afraid that I did something wrong • Afraid I'm in trouble	• Someone scheduled a meeting with me this afternoon and I don't know what it's about yet

---

Going Deeper: Your Fear Self and Your True Self

In Buddhist teachings, there's a saying: "Invite your fear to tea." In other words, the best way to work with your Fear Self is to befriend it. It's a "keep your friends close and your enemies closer" type of approach. You already have a lot of info on your Fear Self and how to identify it: what it sounds like, where it's located, its communication strategies (the Four Os), and how it shows up in your body differently than your True Self. That's more than enough to begin shifting into Directional Living. But it can also be helpful to get to know the personality and profile of your Fear Self in a deeper way; everyone's Fear Self has its own consistent and identifiable patterns.

So go ahead and invite your Fear Self to tea. Spend some time getting up close and personal. To start, give it a name.

1. VISUALIZING AND NAMING YOUR FEAR SELF

Give your Fear Self a full identity. Form a clear picture of your personal Fear Self: personify it, name it, and imagine what it might look like. Maybe you draw it. Maybe you google something and find a picture of it. Make it something funny!

The reason we personify the Fear Self is not to be cute or because I thought this would be a fun hoop for you to jump through. It's because personifying, naming, and visualizing something is the best way for our minds to identify and recognize it, and thus differentiate it from the True Self. Renowned meditation teacher Sharon Salzberg talks about how she imagines this voice as the whiny, crabby Lucy from *Peanuts*. Whenever she hears that voice talking in her head, she pictures Lucy and imagines the cartoon character's high-pitched voice. Salzberg says she starts laughing every time. It's hard to take that voice seriously when it sounds like Lucy admonishing Charlie Brown.

Another favorite example is a client who deemed her Fear Self the voice of Cardi B, in particular in her epic Jimmy Fallon interview— the outfit, the *brrr* noises, the whole thing (google it). Other clients have made their Fear Self the freaky film character Chucky, various gremlins and goblins, and even certain political figures. I encourage you to think of something along these lines that makes it difficult for you to take your Fear Self seriously and that reminds you it's a trigger-happy saboteur of your life. Get creative! This is meant to be fun, and of course, please don't get stuck trying to get it "right." Use the Principle of the First Draft! Your Fear Self, like everything else, is allowed to grow and evolve. You can change your mind.

Next, take this lovely character to "tea" and grill them so that you get to know your Fear Self better than it knows itself.

If your Fear Self were a person or a character:

What would it look like?

What or whom does it sound like?

Now find or draw a picture of your Fear Self. Etch it into your mind and/or keep it somewhere prominent. Describe it briefly here.

_____

_____

_____

_____

Finally, give that Fear Self a name! What will you call your Fear Self?

_____

_____

_____

_____

Moving forward, every time you notice that your Fear Self is getting involved, see it in your mind's eye. Hear it. Greet it by name.

2. THE FEAR SELF INTERVIEW

List at least five examples of Fear Self thoughts.

(If you need inspiration, start with the reasons why you are stuck in your life right now and feel unable to change, and write those down— they're likely to be incarnations of your Fear Self. You can also reference the Four Omens, or any of the other Fear Self key words in this appendix on pages 258–60.)

_____

_____

_____

_____

What are the favorite "tells" of your Fear Self? What are the Omens, the key words, or the beliefs about yourself that it relies on most heavily?

_____

_____

_____

_____

Specifically, what are some of your Fear Self's "signature lines" and go-to intimidation tactics? What is the most common fear that comes up for you?

_____

_____

_____

_____

When is your Fear Self's voice the loudest? Under what conditions is it most likely to appear?

_____

_____

_____

_____

What do you notice when your Fear Self is present? What does it feel like when your Fear Self is around? What does your body feel like? What's the quality of your thoughts? How do you behave and make decisions when your Fear Self is present?

_____

_____

_____

_____

3. MEETING YOUR TRUE SELF: A VISUALIZATION EXERCISE

The same logic of visualizing and naming holds for your True Self, but because the True Self can be a bit harder to detect for UFOAs, I like to do a visualization exercise that's a bit more involved to help bypass the Fear Self.

You may not have answers to all (or any!) of your questions, which is no problem. If that's the case, just leave those blank. There's no right way to do this exercise! Don't put pressure on this activity.

First, get comfortable. If you like, imagine what may entice your True Self to visit you (within your current environment) and do that. And if you don't know what your True Self might like, imagine what one's True Self might like and adopt that scenario. Maybe it's your favorite chair with an iced coffee, or in bed with lots of blankets, or your favorite bench in a park.

Obviously, you can't read and close your eyes at the same time, but you may want to read a sentence or two and then pause and close your eyes and really see what is being suggested in your mind's eye. For many, it deepens the experience.

Now, let your mind take you to your favorite place, real or imagined, a place where you feel completely safe, relaxed, and joyful, where there's no one special you have to be. Try to bring it to life in as much detail as possible. What does it feel like? What does it smell and sound like?

Location: Where were you? Does it have any significance to you? What did it feel like to be in this place? Write down as many notable details as you can remember.

_____

_____

_____

_____

_____

As you walk around and get to know the safe place, you become aware that your True Self is approaching you and there's a sense of excitement in the air. You're about to meet the part of you that knows you completely and has access to all the wisdom and universal intelligence. This is your biggest advocate.

Your Companion: Who did you meet? What was he/she/they/it like? What was he/she/they/it wearing? What did it feel like to be together? Write down as many notable details as you can remember.

_____

_____

_____

_____

_____

Your True Self has all the answers you're seeking. You now have an opportunity to ask your True Self anything that you want to know. I suggest you ask the following questions, plus any others that may come to you, and listen for the answers.

True Self Questions:

What is your name?

_____

What do you know about my Big Direction?

_____

_____

_____

_____

What do I need to know right now?

_____

_____

_____

_____

What do I need to do right now?

_____

_____

_____

_____

What do I need to try?

_____

_____

_____

_____

What do I need to accept or let go of?

_____

_____

_____

_____

Any other questions you'd like to ask:

_____

_____

_____

_____

When you're ready to say goodbye to your True Self, do so, and know that you can come back to this exercise, and your True Self, whenever you like.

Resources for Phase III—Release

Going Deeper: The Life Scan

Since you've already gotten the hang of scanning for HAYWALTs from a concrete outline of your life (your calendar), you can continue to mine for HAYWALTs by scanning each thematic area of your life.

Go through each category that follows and search your inner landscape in that area of your life for anything that has that distinct "colder" feeling to it. Write down anything and everything you can think of that's bugging you, chafing, just feeling not quite right, or feeling totally and completely wrong. These will be the next items on your list of HAYWALTs.

Once you've identified the HAYWALTs, continue by sorting and then deHAYWALTing, as we did with the calendar purge.

Remember that HAYWALTs can be big or small; there are no right or wrong ones, *and* they are entirely subjective.

Career/Current Role/Colleagues/Tasks/Work Environment:

_____

_____

_____

_____

Money/Finances:

_____
_____
_____
_____

Health and Wellness:

_____
_____
_____
_____

Friends/Community:

_____
_____
_____
_____

Family (whatever this means to you):

_____
_____
_____
_____

Significant Other/Partner(s)/Romance:

_____
_____
_____
_____

Personal Growth/Mental and Emotional Health:

_____

_____

_____

_____

Fun/Recreation/Adventure:

_____

_____

_____

_____

Physical Environment/Your Home/Neighborhood/City:

_____

_____

_____

_____

Tips and Tricks—DeHAYWALTing Strategies

Once you've drilled down to your precise HAYWALT, or your best guess for now, there are three main ways to address it: Cancel, Improve, Alternative—or CIA, for short. Another acronym, hooray!

1. **Cancel:** Cancel it, straight up. You're done with this one. Say no to that ski vacation, quit a job, stop hanging out with a specific group of people, get a divorce, move, stop drinking. Just get rid of the damn thing. These are pretty straightforward, which, of course, is not the same as easy.

2. **Improve:** Sometimes it's not aligned to get rid of the thing wholesale, but that doesn't mean you need to accept it as is. You might ask, "Is there a way to improve the situation?" Maybe you go on the ski trip but rent your own house, snowshoe, and meet everyone après-ski instead. Maybe you love your company and your role but loathe your boss—can you improve the situation by changing managers? This might also mean setting a boundary. I had a client in her twenties whose parents were getting divorced. Whenever she saw her mom, her mother spent most of the time trying to get information about her father, badmouthing him, and talking about the divorce. It was a major HAYWALT, so my client, exasperated, just cut her mother off completely—the "cancel" approach. Only, having no contact with her mother became its own HAYWALT. This is a situation where the "improve" approach may be the appropriate one. She could have improved the situation by setting a boundary and sharing with her mother what she was and wasn't available for. Something like, "I miss you, and I want to see you, but I'm not available for any conversations about Dad or the divorce. Everything else is fair game, and I'd love to hear about it." DeHAYWALT complete!

3. **Alternative:** Again, it may not feel aligned to get rid of the whole situation. Is there an alternative, better-feeling way to

achieve the essence of this HAYWALT? Can you trade this HAYWALT for something else that's equal but more aligned? Maybe parties aren't your thing, so instead of attending your friend's big birthday bash, you offer to take them out for lunch instead. Maybe you really don't want to travel during the December holidays, but you'd love to go visit family for New Year's. Perhaps you sit out the ski trip but offer to plan the next group vacation at a beach location where each couple has their own hotel room. Sometimes deHAYWALTing takes a bit of creative resourcefulness.

Resources for Phase V—Iterate

Cheat Sheet: Aligned Action Formula Checklist

1. SCREENSHOT YOUR MIND

Idea:

2. ARTICULATE THE DESIRE (SAY IT OUT LOUD.)

To whom:

3. DO SOME RESEARCH ON IT (GOOGLE IT!)

Key learnings:

4. HAVE A CONVERSATION

With whom:

5. TAKE AN ACTION, ANY ACTION

Next aligned action:

The Directional Dictionary

Alignment:
the desired and primary state of Directional Living, where you're being led by your Inner Navigation System on your own most authentic and Directionally right path of most fulfillment

Big Direction:
your flexible and evolving most aligned North Star and the general high-level direction you're heading in; your Directional purpose

Blind ambition vs. aligned ambition:
blind ambition is the Underfulfilled Overachiever's old fear-based way of moving through the world, driven by external Destinational expectations and devoid of fulfillment; aligned ambition is part of the new Directional approach that is inner-guided and leads to fulfillment

Compulsive achieving:
an Underfulfilled Overachiever symptom characterized by the incessant accumulation of achievements that is driven by the unconscious belief that achievements will provide safety and happiness

Destinational Living/ Destinationalism:
the Underfulfilled Overachiever's approach to life and, in many places, the dominant paradigm, in which one pursues tangible, recognizable destinations based on the lie that this will earn security and happiness

Directional Living:
a new, inner-directed, process-oriented (Directionally oriented) philosophy and framework for a fulfilling life

The EA:
a tool to help Underfulfilled Overachievers become comfortable with letting go of outcomes and control, it imagines a personal assistant, co-creative partner, and personified representative from the universe to

whom you can delegate, ask for help, and trust to manage anything and everything when you feel stuck or uncertain

Fear Self:
our very loud and heavy-handed "survive" part that fears anything new or uncertain, holds us back from our Something Bigger, and obscures our True Self's voice

The Four Omens (Four Os):
the four characteristics of decision-making that indicate unfulfilling, Destinational decisions: Obligation, Objectivity, Optics, and Outcomes

The Fulfillment Ache (F-ache):
the existential chafing that develops when there's an alignment gap, when the distance between who we are and what we truly want, or between the lives we are living and the lives we really want, grows too great for too long; it is nicknamed "the F-ache" (pronounced like *fake*) because Underfulfilled Overachievers are essentially faking it by inhabiting lives that aren't aligned for them

The Fulfillment Test:
the scanning of decision criteria for the Four Omens—Obligation, Objectivity, Optics, and Outcomes—to determine the likelihood of a personally fulfilling trajectory

HAYWALT:
an acronym that stands for "How are you walking around like that?" and describes anything that is consistently weighing you down, holding you back, blocking your True Self, or is out of alignment for you, usually as a result of Destinational Living

Inner Navigation System (INS):
the innate and most essential tool of Directional Living that functions like a GPS powered by your True Self, providing personalized, current, and constantly updating directions guiding you on your most aligned, Directionally right path

The Lily Pad Approach:
a metaphorical approach to the Directional Living practice of being process-oriented rather than outcome-oriented in which you imagine yourself playing a video game where you need to traverse a river by stepping across a path of lily pads, except that only one lily pad appears at a time, so you must take the next step and trust that the subsequent lily pad will appear so that you won't be left stranded

Perfection paralysis:
an Underfulfilled Overachiever symptom characterized by having difficulty making decisions as a result

of the Destinational outsourcing practice of determining the single universally correct, or objectively perfect, choice, according to the court of public opinion

The Principle of Exposure: the first premise of the Directional recovery process that focuses on "exposing" yourself to the content instead of prioritizing "completion," trusting the process of informational osmosis, and allowing your brain to titrate the most important information for you in the right timing

The Principle of the First Draft: the second premise of the Directional recovery process wherein you approach the process as if it were your first draft or just the next "layer of the onion," striving for neither perfection nor completion

Productivity hoarding: an Underfulfilled Overachiever symptom evinced by a preoccupation with being productive at all times and at all costs in an attempt to prove self-worth and ensure safety and security

Programmed vs. pure productivity: programmed productivity, which results in productivity hoarding, is the old Underfulfilled Overachiever way of "doing" that is generated by the external, Destinational, Fear Self–driven belief system, whereas pure productivity is the aligned, Directionally right, True Self–driven way of "doing" that leads to fulfillment

The Purpose Proxy Principle: the Directional tenet that curiosity and joy are the best proxies we have for our "purpose"

To true oneself: the process of restoring your Inner Navigation System to accuracy and recalibrating to align with your True Self and your most Directionally right path

True Self: the inner, innate, most authentic, free-of-external-conditioning core part of each of us that underlies our curiosity, powers our Inner Navigation Systems, and leads the Directional Life

Underfulfilled Overachiever (UFOA): (a) a constant striver who is living a great-on-paper life, has checked all the boxes, done all the "right" things, amassed achievements and external success, yet still feels secretly dissatisfied, unfulfilled, and increasingly disconnected from their work, life, and self; (b) someone who suffers from the foundational belief that achievement is the path to lasting fulfillment; and (c) someone who practices Destinational Living

Reading List

- Beck, Martha:

  - *Finding Your Own North Star: Claiming the Life You Were Meant to Live* (Three Rivers Press, 2001)

  - *The Way of Integrity: Finding the Path to Your True Self* (The Open Field, 2021)

- Ben-Shahar, Tal:

  - *Happier: Learn the Secrets to Daily Joy and Lasting Fulfillment* (McGraw Hill, 2007)

- Brown, Brené:

  - *The Gifts of Imperfection: Let Go of Who You Think You're Supposed to Be and Embrace Who You Are* (Hazelden Publishing, 2010)

  - *Daring Greatly: How the Courage to Be Vulnerable Transforms the Way We Live, Love, Parent, and Lead* (Avery, 2015)

- Burkeman, Oliver:

  - *Four Thousand Weeks: Time Management for Mortals* (Farrar, Straus and Giroux, 2021)

- Burnett, Bill, and Dave Evans:

  - *Designing Your Life: How to Build a Well-Lived, Joyful Life* (Knopf, 2016)

- Cameron, Julia:

  - *The Artist's Way: A Spiritual Path to Higher Creativity* (TarcherPerigee, 2002)

- Chodron, Pema:

  - *When Things Fall Apart: Heart Advice for Difficult Times* (Shambhala Publications, 1997)

- Clear, James:

  - *Atomic Habits: An Easy & Proven Way to Build Good Habits & Break Bad Ones* (Avery, 2018)

- Coelho, Paulo:

  - *The Alchemist* (HarperOne, 1993)

- Cooper, Brittney:

  - *Eloquent Rage: A Black Feminist Discovers Her Superpower* (St. Martin's Press, 2018)

- Doyle, Glennon:

  - *Untamed* (Dial Press, 2020)

- Dweck, Carol S.:

  - *Mindset: The New Psychology of Success* (Ballantine Books, 2006)

- Frankl, Viktor E.:

  - *Man's Search for Meaning* (Beacon Press, 2006)

- García, Héctor, and Francesc Miralles:

  - *Ikigai: The Japanese Secret to a Long and Happy Life* (Penguin Books, 2017)

- Gilbert, Elizabeth:

  - *Big Magic: Creative Living Beyond Fear* (Riverhead Books, 2015)

- Hanh, Thich Nhat:

  - *The Art of Living: Peace and Freedom in the Here and Now* (HarperOne, 2017)

• Hersey, Tricia:

  • *Rest Is Resistance: A Manifesto* (Little, Brown Spark, 2022)

• Horney, Karen:

  • *Feminine Psychology* (W. W. Norton & Company, 1967)

• Kahneman, Daniel:

  • *Thinking, Fast and Slow* (Farrar, Straus and Giroux, 2011)

• Katie, Byron:

  • *Loving What Is: Four Questions That Can Change Your Life* (Harmony, 2002)

• Kimsey-House, Henry, Karen Kimsey-House, Phillip Sandahl, and Laura Whitworth:

  • *Co-Active Coaching: The Proven Framework for Transformative Conversations at Work and in Life* (Nicholas Brealey Publishing, 2018)

• Kondo, Marie:

  • *The Life-Changing Magic of Tidying Up: The Japanese Art of Decluttering and Organizing* (Ten Speed Press, 2014)

• Lamott, Anne:

  • *Bird by Bird: Some Instructions on Writing and Life* (Anchor Books, 1995)

• LaPorte, Danielle:

  • *The Desire Map: A Guide to Creating Goals with Soul* (Sounds True, 2014)

• Lorde, Audre:

  • *Sister Outsider: Essays and Speeches* (Crossing Press, 2007)

- *The Selected Works of Audre Lorde* (W. W. Norton & Company, 2020)

- McBride, Hillary L.:

  - *The Wisdom of Your Body: Finding Healing, Wholeness, and Connection through Embodied Living* (Central Recovery Press, 2020)

- Miller, Alice:

  - *The Drama of the Gifted Child: The Search for the True Self* (Basic Books, 1997)

- Nagoski, Emily, and Amelia Nagoski:

  - *Burnout: The Secret to Unlocking the Stress Cycle* (Ballantine Books, 2019)

- Newport, Cal:

  - *Deep Work: Rules for Focused Success in a Distracted World* (Grand Central Publishing, 2016)

- Nichtern, Ethan:

  - *The Road Home: A Contemporary Exploration of the Buddhist Path* (North Point Press, 2015)

- Odell, Jenny:

  - *How to Do Nothing: Resisting the Attention Economy* (Melville House, 2019)

- Petersen, Anne Helen:

  - *Can't Even: How Millennials Became the Burnout Generation* (Houghton Mifflin Harcourt, 2020)

- Ruiz, Don Miguel:

  - *The Four Agreements: A Practical Guide to Personal Freedom* (Amber-Allen Publishing, 1997)

READING LIST

- Rumi (as translated by Coleman Barks):

    - *The Essential Rumi* (HarperOne, 1995)

- Schwartz, Richard C.:

    - *No Bad Parts: Healing Trauma & Restoring Wholeness with the Internal Family Systems Model* (Sounds True, 2021)

- Tippett, Krista:

    - *Becoming Wise: An Inquiry into the Mystery and Art of Living* (Penguin Press, 2017)

- Truitt, Anne:

    - *Daybook: The Journal of an Artist* (Pantheon Books, 1982)

- Tulshyan, Ruchika, and Jodi-Ann Burey:

    - "Stop Telling Women They Have Imposter Syndrome" (*Harvard Business Review*, February 11, 2021)

- Whyte, David:

    - *The Heart Aroused: Poetry and the Preservation of Soul in Corporate America* (Crown Currency, 1996)

    - *The Three Marriages: Reimagining Work, Self and Relationships* (Riverhead Books, 2010)